Walking in Line

"It is my honor to endorse Dr. James Croone's book *Walking in Line*. We have had a long friendship, and although I serve James as his pastor, he serves me as a coach and mentor, especially as it relates to racial tension and ethnic bias. Dr. Croone is articulate, well studied, and has personally lived what he teaches in this book. I have seen firsthand his patience and kindness, and at the same time his unswerving commitment to truth and justice. I am very proud of this work but prouder to call him my friend. You will be a better pastor, leader, Christian, and person for reading this book."

—**DONALD E. ROSS**, network leader,
Northwest Ministry Network

"In his new book, *Walking in Line*, Dr. James Croone writes with surgical precision and clarity. Doctor visits are opportunities for honest revelation of pain and struggle and to receive examination, diagnosis, and treatment. The responsibility lies with the patient to accept and apply the doctor's orders. Too often we have rejected the truth and grace of the gospel and favored instead a culturally comfortable Christian ethic on reconciliation. All sincere readers will be healed of bias if they walk the line of Christ's gospel."

—**WALTER HARVEY**, president, National Black
Fellowship of the Assemblies of God

"My good friend Dr. James Croone has provided a profound yet simple resource for beckoning the church to racial reconciliation, justice, mercy, and grace. While soundly nailing the hinge to the door of biblical truth, he also opens it slowly and methodically, to reveal a clear line forward. Along the way you encounter the realization of your own biases. That self-awareness leads to hope and courage through stories, historical facts, theology, and more practical steps to implement in your own heart, family, church, and neighborhood. *Walking in Line* asks powerful questions that will stimulate your thinking and touch your heart. Together, we can change our world."

—DON DETRICK, associate network leader,
Northwest Ministry Network

"Dr. Croone begins with a powerful question: 'Why do many believers who profess faith in God harbor biases against other ethnic groups?' His answer, 'Because it is a heart issue,' sets the foundation for seven transformative lessons designed to engage the heart for change. These lessons delve into how our flesh, entrenched biases, resistance to change, and desire for comfort obstruct the biblical ministry of reconciliation and the church's multicultural mandate. Each lesson concludes with thought-provoking questions that prompt readers to ponder, reflect, and take action. This teaching is crucial for us all, especially in these divided times, and I am pleased to strongly recommend this book."

—STEVE IGNELL, retired scientist, NOAA Fisheries

"Dr. James Croone's latest book, *Walking in Line: Dealing with Bias in Light of the Gospel*, accurately prescribes the biblical solution for racial reconciliation—not just in America but for people in every nation. Dr. Croone has a strong grasp of American history without ignoring the sin of intentional systemic racism that enslaved Africans for centuries and decimated the indigenous populations of the North American continent through European colonization. He points out that only the biblical perspective is the path to forgiveness, reconciliation, and love between people of all races and cultures. This book is a must read for those who want to move forward in loving their neighbor."

—NATHANIEL J. MULLEN, pastor,
Victorious Life Christian Center

Walking in Line

Dealing with Bias in Light of the Gospel

JAMES D. CROONE SR.

Foreword by L. William Oliverio Jr.

WIPF & STOCK · Eugene, Oregon

Wipf & Stock
An Imprint of Wipf and Stock Publishers
199 W. 8th Ave., Suite 3
Eugene, OR 97401

www.wipfandstock.com

PAPERBACK ISBN: 979-8-3852-3801-9
HARDCOVER ISBN: 979-8-3852-3802-6
EBOOK ISBN: 979-8-3852-3803-3

VERSION NUMBER 03/26/25

Photo Credit for Cover: De'Aires Berry

Henry, Mary T. "Martin Luther King Jr. Arrives for His Only Seattle Visit on November 8, 1961." History Link. Jan. 8, 1999. Creative Commons.

Seedbed. "Xavier's Powerful Story About Race and Reconciliation: Awakening Stories." Apr. 2, 2019. https://seedbed.com/xaviers-powerful-story-about-race-and-reconciliation-awakening-stories/. Used by Permission.

Williams, Marvin, and Al Lopus. "A True Story of Prejudice, Forgiveness, and True Reconciliation." Best Christian Workplaces. June 23, 2020. https://work-places.org/articles/flourish-factor/healthy-communication/a-true-story-of-prejudice-forgiveness-and-true-reconciliation. Used by Permission.

To my readers,
who find themselves in these pages
and enact positive change.

Contents

Foreword

THOSE OF US WHO follow Jesus of Nazareth and identify with the people of God in the church can look at our vast global history with both joy and sorrow. The church, with around 2.4 billion people who identify as Christian worldwide today, has had many historical situations where our witness has shined and we have embodied—though, even in our best instances, not without problems and hurts, sins and harm—the inbreaking of the kingdom of God into the here and now. In other situations, we must confess. In far too many situations in history, Christian churches and communities have been overrun by cultural sins, cruelties, and other failures to understand and live up to the truth and meaning of the gospel. Like chronic individual sin, chronic corporate sin is destructive for human lives.

For US Christians, the four hundred year history of racism resides at the top of the list of chronic corporate and individual sin. Sadly, racism and harmful racialized attitudes, assumptions, and practices continue to be normal, even as there has been much progress in terms of changed hearts and social as well as legal norms in US society. Racist treatment of anyone and perhaps especially our fellow Christians should cut us to the heart.

The long-term trauma and socialization from racist treatment is damaging in psychological, practical, financial, moral, and many other ways. Racism and racist treatment of others have not only been accepted by but have even found aid, comfort, and promotion in American churches—from the days before Emancipation from slavery, through to the Jim Crow era, during and beyond the era of the Civil Rights Movement, and up to the present day. Those who professed Christ stood at the forefront of abolitionist and emancipatory movements, inspired by Jesus and the biblical prophets. Concurrently, professing Christians also defended enslaving, oppressive, and demeaning laws, social structures, and daily practices. They wittingly or unwittingly took on roles more akin to the *oppressors* in Scripture—displaying characteristics more like Pharaoh's grasping for power and wealth or Pilate's political maneuvering than *Spirit-led exemplars* who countered them with the power, righteousness, and love of God.

It may feel quite tempting to think that this is all simply behind us, yet ethnic and racial and dehumanizing hatreds have long-standing roots in corporate social and individual sinfulness, in social habits and in sinful human nature. Their continuing effects still ripple through cultures, families, personal and corporate psychologies, and more. Sometimes those of us from majority groups feel shocked when we see the degrading and humiliating things a friend from an ethnic or racial minority group goes through in day-to-day life.

When I was a college freshman at a Christian university in the Midwest in the 1990s, a black friend down the hall came up to me visibly angry and hurt; he was holding a piece of paper with a racial slur on it that someone had placed underneath the windshield wiper of his car parked at the school.

A couple of years later, friends gathered to hear the hurt of a student leader and resident advisor who had sat in the car and watched his decorated military veteran father humiliated by police in harsh treatment during a traffic stop in a rural area that had a reputation for targeting black drivers.

Some years back, my stepfather, a native of El Salvador and the lead engineer for two decades on the landing gear for a dozen or so major commercial and military aircraft, was taking my family out for a Good Friday fish fry. We could not get seated for an oddly long time, and our young children were having a hard time waiting; when my white mother went to the hostess, we were seated immediately.

In the urban midwestern culture where I grew up in the 1980 and 1990s, most every ethnic group was the butt of some kind of ethnic joke or stereotype; for some reason the Poles were the main targets in my neighborhood. These jokes were most often based on degrading stereotypes that influenced our perceptions of our neighbors of that ethnicity.

When I was about ten years old, my mother and I were sitting down at a church fellowship dinner, and I was sitting with a black friend from Sunday school. Excited to see another friend, I invited him to sit by us, but he refused because, as he told me, using an insult to do so, that there were too many black people at that table. Most of us have stories of our own and from friends and colleagues of such personal insult and demeaning experiences that occurred along racial lines.

I share these stories not because they are anywhere near the most serious instances of racism or because I want to rehearse instances I have known all that much but rather because *they have been so normal for so many.* You and I and most of the people we know have stories along these lines. I apologize if illustrating the daily hurts brings up past or current wounds here. However, this is part of the cost of addressing this issue to bring about healing.

What remains so negatively powerful is the broad social norming of racism—from the subtle yet powerful demeaning acts to violence inflicted along racial lines, to the long-term effects of racial trauma, to the legacies of segregation and redlining, to discriminatory hiring practices and other social norms of disrespect.

Racism is an affront to the biblical witness concerning humanity. In the face of ancient ethnic hatreds, enslavement practices, killing, dehumanizing of others, and more, the Hebrew Bible names humans as the image of God—his emblem on earth, who share somehow in God's very likeness; humans are God's stewards on earth, each with inherent dignity.

Of course, humans are so often motivated by self-interest, and considering one's own ethnic or racial group as superior to others is a way of indulging in a social strategy of elevating one group at the expensive harm of others, whether one is conscious of this or not. Yet, the command of the Lord could not be clearer: *Love your neighbor as yourself* (Lev 19:18; Matt 19:19, 22:39; Mark 12:31, 33; Luke 10:27; Rom 13:19; Gal 5:14; Jas 2:8).

Elevating one's ethnic, racial, or social group above others in ways that do deep harm to others constitutes an abject failure to follow the Great Commandment, as loving God with our whole being directly connects to loving our neighbor. Christians are called to participate in the inbreaking of the kingdom of God in the here and now; even if its fullness has not yet come, God's reign and rule is already present among us.

The Spirit, who ushers the kingdom of God into our hearts, lives, and communities, is the great transformer. Paul tells the Corinthians that the Spirit will transform them into the fullness of the image of God, who is the Lord Jesus: "And we all, who with unveiled faces contemplate the Lord's glory, are being transformed into his image with ever-increasing glory, which comes from the Lord, who is the Spirit" (2 Cor 3:18 NIV). The Spirit changes us into the likeness of our Lord Jesus. It is an act of transformative grace for us to live out the deep trust in God that we find in the Sermon on the Mount, to live out the radical love we see in Jesus's parables in Luke, and to exhibit the fruit of the Spirit that Paul lists in Gal 5. The Spirit can and will transform us if we stay open to the power and love of God. The Word of God in the Scriptures is also powerfully transformative. The ancient church father Irenaeus of Lyons referred to the Word and the Spirit as the two hands of the Father.[1]

In this volume, my friend, James Croone, takes you on a journey through biblical passages that will enliven your heart by the Spirit. He compares the Scriptures to the line that God has laid down for us to measure our own attitudes and beliefs, to test our own biases and assumptions. We all have biases and assumptions, but the question is whether we have those that are good, helpful, and in line with God's good purposes for the world.

Each of us sins, fails, and remains in need of growth. We are merely finite human beings who live in a certain time and place, and we need our perspectives challenged by Scripture all the time.

---

1. Irenaeus, *Against Heresies*, 5.6.1.

God can transform any of our interpretive assumptions that are out of step with the Spirit to those that exhibit the fruit of the Spirit.

This book challenges me—not only because it offers biblical wisdom to correct what needs to be continually corrected in us about these matters but because of the kindness, wisdom, and love with which these corrections are made. James does not sugarcoat things, yet he speaks with a tone of unity, healing, and peace.

This book is good biblical theology, and it communicates in understandable and helpful ways. Each chapter culminates with a prayer that appropriates the content to our own lives to help internalize the message and open us up to what God would have us do. Perhaps our closing prayer, together, could be that the church in America and the global church might allow the Word and Spirit to transform and heal us so that future generations can say that, in the face of historical errors, we corrected course, that we followed the line the Scriptures set out before us and lived as agents of God's healing in the world.

In the story of the good Samaritan (Luke 10:25–37), the wounded man on the road to Jericho would have been presumed to be a fellow Jew. Two religious Jews failed to stop to help this dying man while the ethnically and religiously different Samaritan demonstrated sacrificial love of neighbor. The point the original audience would have readily had in mind, as those who walked those roads, is this—*that wounded and dying man might have been me, and my life might have depended on that Samaritan man stopping, tending to me, and sacrificing for me.* Jesus concludes the story with these words: "Which of these three do you think was a neighbor to the man who fell into the hands of robbers?"

The expert in the law replied, "The one who had mercy on him."

Jesus told him, "Go and do likewise" (Luke 10:36–37).

—L. William (Bill) Oliverio Jr.
Associate Professor of Public Theology,
Northwest University, Kirkland, Washington
Coeditor of *Pneuma: The Journal of the*
Society for Pentecostal Studies

Preface

As a black American, I can speak to many of the dismays of racism, and I can express my hurt as a black Christian when I see biases among my brothers and sisters in Christ—white, black, or otherwise). Through my years of being a professor in Bible colleges and pastoring, it perplexes me how one can hold on to biases against those of other ethnicities and proudly proclaim to be a follower of Jesus Christ. However, this has always been a standard fixture throughout the history of those who have interpreted the word of God to enslave, oppress, and extort those made in his image. One would only believe that through all the advanced developments made in studies of resources, archeology, and linguistics analysis—and, most importantly, being in tune with God's Spirit—that we would have an even better grasp of the gospel, ridding ourselves of these pseudo-interpretations.

I would be less than genuine if I were to say that much of the televised news reports nationwide over the past years exposing the injustices done to black Americans has not infuriated me or made me want to scream. However, I recognize that I am God's servant first, and his word guides my actions and thoughts. Especially in times of chaos and turmoil, "God is [my] refuge and strength, a very present help in trouble" (Ps 46:1 KJV). I find no solace in media, publications, or friends with opinions, all of which tend to lead favorably toward external fixes. Much of what has been touted conveys solutions that are irrational and fueled by anger and reprisal. Civil unrest, reforms, laws, and financial retribution are short-lived solutions; bias is an internal problem. No matter how stringent laws are, there are always loopholes. There are no loopholes internally, though, if one truly walks in line with the gospel. I pray that this book assists in transforming the hearts of those wrestling with bias and leads them to the path of restoration.

Acknowledgments

I MUST START BY thanking my primary supporters—my wife, Bobbie Croone, and my mother, Charlotte Croone, for their constant encouragement and unwavering support for me to follow God's call to pastoral ministry. I would be remiss not to thank my fellow laborers in Christ who contributed their time reading this manuscript and offering great advice and constructive criticism: Don Detrick, Don Ross, Steve Ignell, Juri Hobbs, Joel Arthur, Daniel Nordblad, and Jason Dick.

Introduction

"His people have a tendency toward unfaithfulness—toward worshipping other gods, and they go through cycles of disobedience leading to judgement, leading to repentance, and return. Yet despite the repeated acts of unfaithfulness, God has remained faithful to His often-unfaithful people."

—JEFF SYVERSON[1]

ONE OF HIS MOST famous songs, "I Walk the Line," details Johnny Cash's values and lifestyle. It was a promise to remain faithful to his first wife, Vivian Liberto, while he was on the road. Cash was twenty-two when he married Vivian on August 7, 1954; their daughter Rosanne was born ten months later. Cash got a taste of temptation later in 1955 when he signed with Sun Records. He released two singles for the label that year and toured with their star, Elvis Presley, who attracted throngs of female fans at every stop. Cash wrote "I Walk the Line" as a reminder to stay true, which it turned out was not very easy to do. When the song took off, he became a star and was suddenly enveloped in distractions and vice. Constantly touring, Cash was rarely home. In 1956, he met June Carter at the Grand Ole Opry; in the early 1960s, they started

1. Syverson, "Faithful to the Unfaithful."

working together and kindled an affair. Vivian filed for divorce in 1966; it was finalized a year later, and, in 1968, Cash and Carter got married. That one took; they were together until June's death in 2003. "It was kind of a prodding to myself to, 'Play it straight, Johnny,'" Cash said of the song.[2]

Although this book's title, *Walking in Line*, is based on Galatians 2:11–14,[3] the premise mirrors the meaning of Cash's predicament. The phrase walking in line means "to maintain a fragile balance between one extreme and another"—"good and evil, sanity and insanity, decency and decadence," and "to behave" or "to abide by moral standards," "to walk a straight path of decency by following the rules," to "walk the straight and narrow."[4] Or, in our case, as believers, we walk in line with God's statutes and obey his rules.

Whereas Johnny Cash's hit song details his bout with temptation and infidelity, we too are guilty of succumbing to types of unfaithfulness—namely, against God—which brings to mind the phrase spiritual adultery. In many ways, we have kindled an affair with worldviews, cultures, and traditions.[5] In Jer 3:20, the Lord describes spiritual adultery as equivalent to the unfaithfulness of one's spouse: "Surely, as a treacherous wife leaves her husband, so have you been treacherous to me, O house of Israel, declares the Lord." Consequently, we have not always walked in line with Lord or heeded Jesus's command to love one another and overcome our biases.

Ultimately, we can point to many things that anger, confuse, and sadden us about the state of the racial divide in the world. If we are not careful, we will become bitter and resentful of those we deem indifferent to pursuing a way forward in rectifying the racial

2. Winkler, "'I Walk the Line,'" para. 12.

3. See lesson 4.

4. *Urban Dictionary*, s.v. "walk the line," last udated July 9, 2006, https://www.urbandictionary.com/define.php?term=Walk%20the%20line.

5. In no way is this statement implying that cultures and traditions are wrong in themselves. When they supersede God's word, though, they are an affront to his nature.

issues we face today. However, the truth is, many do not know the path ahead. Great books have been written on racial reconciliation, but they often fall flat on how to move forward, leaving the reader wondering, What now? I have spoken to numerous pastors, influential acquaintances, and friends about *what now*.

First and foremost, racial reconciliation or reconstruction is not an external problem; like most laws or regulations, there is both ambiguity and inadequacy, which produce loopholes. Therefore, the only other solution involves turning inward to the internal aspects of this problem. One may argue that the heart can be untrustworthy, and they would be right. The Bible wholeheartedly stands in agreement with this sentiment. Jesus speaks of this condition:

> For from within, out of a person's heart, come evil thoughts, sexual immorality, theft, murder, adultery, greed, wickedness, deceit, lustful desires, envy, slander, pride, and foolishness. All these vile things come from within; they are what defile you. (Mark 7:21–23 NLT)

This list is exhaustive and gets to the very root of our ills. Fear and anger feed prejudice, which in all cases manifests itself cruelly. Scripture informs us that if we allow our minds to dwell on envy, hate, and irrationality, those things will ultimately lead to sin. Evil things come from within, so how do we tackle this issue?

We start with the heart. Throughout the following lessons, you will answer thought-provoking questions that trigger your mind (intellect, reason, and thoughts). The heart houses the intangible parts of your being (hopes, desires, and emotions). Ephesians 2:8–10 says we are saved through faith. The biblical term faith in Greek is *pistis*, which means trust, confidence in, or assurance.[6] Therefore, the mind and heart play an active role in faith. To have faith in God, one must believe and trust God. Believing involves the mind, and trusting involves the heart; so why do many believers who profess faith in God harbor biases against other ethnic groups? Because it is a heart issue. Love is a powerful

6. Bible Hub, "Pistis."

emotion. Trust is the confidence you have in someone who will always be loyal to you and love you. Hence our faith in God; if this declaration is correct, 1 John 4:20 says if one hates their brother, they should question their love for God. "If someone says, 'I love God,' but hates a fellow believer, that person is a liar; for if we don't love people we can see, how can we love God, whom we cannot see?" (NLT). I hope this book will serve as a guide to articulate an outline toward positive change. Ultimately, it is the work of the Holy Spirit to transform the individual, and that is my prayer.

CHAPTER ANALYSIS

Lesson 1: Kingdom of Reconciliation Analysis (2 Cor 5:16–21)

In lesson 1, we learn that the flesh plays a vital role in hindering the process of reconciliation. By taking a closer look at Paul's conversion, we will find that Paul's upbringing in a biased-laden home not only contaminated his perception of those who were non-Jews but carried over into his adult life. Not until conversion did he learn that once-held biases and standards no longer exist because a new appreciation for Christ and others had come.

Lesson 2: A Call to Justice and Mercy (Acts 6:1–7)

In lesson 2, we see a clear example of discrimination in the early church. There was a blatant disregard for a group (Hellenists) who were seen as outcasts and not entitled to fairness. The *privileged* faction (Hebrews) imposing this indifference, prided themselves on their heritage. Although both groups had zeal for the Lord, the sin of pride threatened to impede the work of the Holy Spirit in the early church. God calls us as believers today, as he did with the faithful leaders of old, to identify with the pain of the marginalized and answer the call for justice and mercy.

Lesson 3: The Wall of Hostility (Eph 2:14–18)

In lesson 3, we look at the metaphorical walls dividing our society and the church. To help grasp the strength of these walls, we examine the historical ramifications of not repeating them in our present churches and community. Unchecked biases have a way of setting up unhealthy boundaries. Therefore, unless we accept Jesus's work on the cross and relinquish all bitterness, pride, and hostility, we will never know what it is like to walk in the fullness of Christ and be free from biases.

Lesson 4: Walking in Line with the Gospel (Gal 2:11–14)

Lesson 4 introduces us to a somewhat partisan account of an admired apostle undermining the gospel he was appointed to uphold. In no way does this discredit his position. However, it reminds us that we, as believers, are not exempt from sin. Discomfort with other cultures is natural, but the question is how we deal with that uneasiness. Being received into a group's comfort space is an opportunity to fellowship, learn, and exemplify the gospel message. To squander such a blessing involves not *walking in line* with the gospel.

Lesson 5: Who Is My Neighbor? (Luke 10:25–37)

We delve into a well-known and often touted Bible passage in lesson 5. Rather than focusing on the primary characters and their failure to assist a wounded traveler, we examine a question posed by a scribe to Jesus: *Who is my neighbor?* The term neighbor carries with it profound associations. These associations are not only homogeneous but require stepping out of your comfort zone and being neighborly to those who do not share your particular standards or opinions—they requre looking past biases that have divided our communities and churches for so long.

Lesson 6: The Cost (Luke 14:25–34)

Lesson 6 begins with a very telling story of a visit to Seattle from the great civil rights leader Dr. Martin Luther King Jr. His story is a perfect segue into the cost of following Christ in tumultuous times. The world rotates on an axis of public opinion, politics, and self-interest. Therefore, change is unavoidable despite the fact that some desire their environment and situation to stay the same. Also, in this lesson, we assess the priorities of the body of Christ (the church) as it pertains to justice and discerning what is the right approach.

Lesson 7: The End Result (Rev 7:9–12)

Lesson 7 presents a sharp distinction between the great multitude—all tribes and peoples and languages standing before the throne—and our present church epoch. Admittedly, there is a semblance of diversity in many churches throughout the Western sphere. However, it befits us as followers of Christ to build authentic relationships with our neighbors—meaning anyone, despite nationality, culture, or social standing. In other words, anyone God places on our footpath. Lesson 7 clarifies the misfortunes of assimilation and sheds light on the importance of valuing the uniqueness of diversity.

WHO IS THIS BOOK FOR?

I hope this book will help believers and nonbelievers alike, as well as church leaders, congregants, and individuals wrestling with cultural biases. I have also attempted to structure this book in an easy-to-read format. It is not theologically dense so as not to bog down the intended message of the lessons. I encourage small groups, specialty courses, and seminary students to consider this for supplemental reading. In short, this book is for anyone willing to *walk in line* with the gospel.

HOW TO USE THIS BOOK

Each lesson includes the following components:

Space for notes: Notetaking is encouraged, and writing helps one remember essential truths that come to mind.

Quotes: Hearing from gifted wordsmiths on various topics is always helpful. Not only does it condense subjects and issues to a bite-size morsel, but it also illuminates thought. Quotes are explicitly used in this book for that very reason, and as a way to segue into a lesson that I pray will have the same effect.

Something to ponder: There are truths throughout the lesson that may require you to ponder or think carefully, particularly before making a decision or reaching a conclusion.

Reflection: Serious thoughts and considerations will appear from time to time in these lessons, strategically placed to suggest unhurried consideration of something called to one's attention earlier.

Response: These lessons are designed to provoke thought. Your answers cannot necessarily be viewed as good or bad because the answers are undoubtedly your feelings. Whether in a group setting or personal reading, it is imperative to self-evaluate honestly and have a balanced, realistic view of yourself. As the apostle Paul writes, "Be honest in your evaluation of yourselves, measuring yourselves by the faith God has given us" (Rom 12:3b NLT).

Prayer: Each lesson ends with a prayer. These prayers are like small pieces of wood (kindling), starting the fire with the expectation of setting a foundation upon which the reader will add the main firewood.

Scripture references: As a rule of thumb, it would be beneficial for you, the reader, to acquaint yourself with the surrounding texts of the central passages. This will enable you to interpret the author's intended meaning correctly.[7]

Glossary: A glossary at the end of the book will assist you with unfamiliar industry-specific words.

---

7. Unless otherwise noted, all Scriptures are taken from the New International Version (NIV).

"So from now on we regard no one from a worldly point of view. Though we once regarded Christ in this way, we do so no longer. Therefore, if anyone is in Christ, the new creation has come: The old has gone, the new is here! All this is from God, who reconciled us to himself through Christ and gave us the ministry of reconciliation: that God was reconciling the world to himself in Christ, not counting people's sins against them. And he has committed to us the message of reconciliation. We are therefore Christ's ambassadors, as though God were making his appeal through us. We implore you on Christ's behalf: Be reconciled to God. God made him who had no sin to be sin for us, so that in him we might become the righteousness of God." (2 Cor 5:16–21)

Lesson 1

Kingdom of Reconciliation

Lord, come into our brokenness and our
lives with your love that heals all.[1]

Xavier Brandon is a leader from Vertical Church ATL
in Atlanta. This past year, at New Room Conference, he
attended the racial reconciliation panel and was challenged by the Holy Spirit to act.

Xavier felt compelled by the Spirit to pray for those
in the aisles after the panel, *seeking reconciliation.* The
first thing he thought to do is a step we all need to take
continually. He prayed that God would remove any un-
intended or subconscious prejudices he held due to his
own past experiences.

Then, *as soon as he was done praying,* God brought
the next step to him. An older white gentleman ap-
proached asking for Xavier to pray for him. The man
told Xavier,

---

1. Morrison, *Be the Bridge*, 11, quoted in Morrison, "June 2020," para. 5.

"I grew up in a church that, they would preach over the pulpit that black people had no souls. I didn't want to believe it, but I grew up and never had an affinity for, and never reached out to, another black person, before. And I was wondering if you could pray for me."

So, Xavier prayed—boldly. He prayed into the man the truth that he is a new creation and prayed against any wickedness residing in him. The power of this prayer that God spoke through Xavier was clear. He describes that there was something visibly different, that even "[the man's] countenance had changed."[2]

Second Corinthians 5:16–21 gives a clear depiction of Paul's life. Key terms, such as *flesh*, *reconciliation*, and *righteousness* illuminate much of this passage. His description of pre- and postconversion offers transparency and a godly perspective toward one another despite differences or ethnicity.

FLESH

Like Paul, we too had a fleshly point of view regarding Christ and others before conversion. Though our innate nature is rooted in sin, learned behavior is a basis of how we conduct ourselves in our surroundings. For instance, Paul's parents were Pharisees (Acts 23:6) and, being strict adherents of the law of Moses, protected themselves, as well as their children, from the uncleanness of gentiles. Their prejudice against non-Jews came naturally due to the elevation of their traditions over the commandments of God (Mark 7:7–9). The cleanliness of the heart was a much lesser concern than their outer cleanliness. These values are found in the behavioral patterns of the Pharisees throughout Scripture. Differences in religion, race, and culture were the primary source of the enmity between the Jews and gentiles. Though God chose Israel to be his people to be a blessing to others, the Jews embraced their cultural practices and ceremonies—not to mention their bloodline

2. Seedbed, "Xavier's Powerful Story," para. 1–5 (emphasis and brackets original).

that tied them to their forefathers, Abraham, Isaac, and Jacob—as separating them from non-Jews. This eventually led to the pharisaical approach of treating the gentiles as second-class citizens. These biases were ingrained into the psyche of Paul as an adolescent, which gave rise to a religious terrorist with racial biases (Phil 3:5–6). "Pharisees are exclusive. They pick and choose who enters the group. But Jesus never valued exclusivity."[3]

We not only have the example of his motley crew of disciples with various occupations and checkered pasts, but added to their number were those who would ultimately deny and betray Him, not to mention a former Pharisee who had vowed to persecute all who chose to follow Jesus. As Andrew David Naselli notes, "Since Paul's conversion, he views people not primarily in terms of ethnicity but according to their relation to Jesus the Messiah. The Jew-Gentile division is now less important for him than the believer-unbeliever distinction."[4] Despite any behavior—learned or otherwise—God alters the fabric of our thinking and reconstructs our lives once true regeneration occurs, which in turn changes how we perceive Christ and others. Once-held biases and standards no longer exist; a new appreciation for Christ and others has come.

Something to Ponder:
The *flesh* plays a vital role in hindering the process
of reconciliation. This can be seen in many facets
of life: family, marriages, politics, racism, etc.

Next Steps: Coming to Jesus is a surreal experience. We are transformed and equipped to become ministers of reconciliation, which enables us to repair any damage we may have caused in our relationship with God or others. Although we are now at peace with God, we are blessed with the responsibility to live at peace with others. Though the Bible does not tell us that Paul made amends

3. Powell, "12 Signs," no. 11.
4. Naselli, "2 Corinthians 5:16," loc. 8682.

with the family and friends of those he persecuted, his walk after he was converted was a testimony itself. However, chances are he had to encounter those he had wronged or their loved ones and had to reconcile those relationships, whether he was directly or indirectly responsible for their imprisonment or death.

RECONCILIATION

Paul's hatred toward the gentiles before his conversion runs in a solid parallel line to how Black America regards the slave trade and Jim Crow laws. This maltreatment has made it hard for Black Americans to fathom the idea of reconciliation. Often, we face moments of reconciliation with family, friends, or those we deem to be close to us. However, according to the *Oxford Dictionary*, reconciliation is "the action of restoring estranged people or parties to friendship: the result; the fact being reconciled."[5] This broadens the definition of those we perceive as the proverbial other, the alienated or distanced. This type of reconciliation (*diallasso*) is seen in Matt 5:24: "Leave your gift there before the altar and go. First, be reconciled to your brother, and then come and offer your gift" (ESV). The term brother (*adelphos*) refers to "a fellow man" or "of the exact nature." However, The Greek term used in 2 Cor 5:19 is *katallasso*, meaning "to change toward, one person toward another or someone."[6] This reconciliation is not *diallasso*, which refers to a mutual change. This can be seen clearly in v. 19, which states, "God was reconciling the world to himself." Since God is holy, humankind are the ones to blame. Therefore, this type of reconciliation does not imply a mutual or shared change but does denote transition: to change one's feelings toward, to reconcile oneself, to become reconciled. To accept or come to terms with something, one must deal with the especially undesirable, difficult, or troubling situation or set of circumstances.

---

5. *Oxford English Dictionary*, s.v. "reconciliation," https://www.oed.com/search/dictionary/?scope=Entries&q=reconciliation&tl=true.

6. *Hebrew-Greek Key Word Study Bible*, s.v. "katallasso," 2448.

RIGHTEOUSNESS

The word *righteousness* comes from a root word that means "straightness." It refers to a state that conforms to an authoritative standard. In the Old Testament, the term *righteousness* is used to define our relationship with God and with other people.[7] As one who eventually realized that all his righteous acts (pre-conversion) were like filthy rags (Isa 64:4), Paul implores us on behalf of Christ to be reconciled to God. Then and only then will we acquire true righteousness through the cleansing of sin by Jesus Christ and the Holy Spirit.

RESPONSE

Describe the homogeneity of your community of faith. Describe the evangelistic efforts to other ethnicities or the lack thereof.

_____

_____

_____

_____

_____

_____

_____

What are some of the perspectives you had that have changed since your conversion? What are some of the biases you have abandoned since your conversion?

_____

_____

_____

_____

7. Youngblood, *Illustrated Bible Dictionary*, 986.

_____

_____

_____

What steps could you take in the area of reconciliation with (a) yourself, (b) God, and (c) those outside your demographic?

_____

_____

_____

_____

_____

_____

_____

What types of biases do you have toward others, either learned as an adolescent, experienced, or practiced?

_____

_____

_____

_____

_____

_____

Pursuing righteousness means turning away from sin and toward Christ and his perfect, righteous ways. How does this look in shedding deeply held biases?

_____

_____

_____

_____

_____

_____

_____

PRAY

Lord, I pray for divine strength and spiritual endurance right now. Even though my outward self is perishing, my inward self is renewed daily. Lord, I believe that you make all things new; therefore, each day, I am renewed by your Holy Spirit. I will not become distracted by my situation. Instead, I will use this pressure to help me become more like you and remain on the path of righteousness. Amen.

In those days when the number of disciples was increasing, the Hellenistic Jews among them complained against the Hebraic Jews because their widows were being overlooked in the daily distribution of food. So the Twelve gathered all the disciples together and said, "It would not be right for us to neglect the ministry of the word of God in order to wait on tables. Brothers and sisters, choose seven men from among you who are known to be full of the Spirit and wisdom. We will turn this responsibility over to them and will give our attention to prayer and the ministry of the word.

This proposal pleased the whole group. They chose Stephen, a man full of faith and of the Holy Spirit; also Philip, Procorus, Nicanor, Timon, Parmenas, and Nicolas from Antioch, a convert to Judaism. They presented these men to the apostles, who prayed and laid their hands on them.

So the word of God spread. The number of disciples in Jerusalem increased rapidly, and a large number of priests became obedient to the faith. (Acts 6:1–7)

Lesson 2

A Call to Justice and Mercy

*Integration begins the day after the minds
of the people are desegregated.*[1]

IT IS NEARLY IMPOSSIBLE for one to come to a place of genuine
coexistence with others if they are facing opposition with the idea
of unification. However, by mastering our biases one can, with
fairness (justice), come to a place of understanding (mercy).

> One year at our church, I was teaching the Old Testament
> book of Malachi. The sermon series was called "Reset." In
> the next-to-last message, we were resetting justice: "Cor-
> recting injustice in the world begins with God correcting
> injustice in me."
>
> After the service, a man came up and said he need-
> ed to ask me to forgive him. "When you were introduced
> as the candidate for senior teaching pastor, I didn't vote
> for you."

1. Horsford, "School Integration," 257–75.

9

"I'm sure many people didn't vote for me," I said, hoping to reassure him.

"You need to know *why* I didn't vote for you," he replied. I continued to listen. He told me that because of some past experiences in his life he had developed a spirit of prejudice and racism against Black people. In essence, he was saying he didn't vote for me because I was Black.

As we stood together, he began to weep and asked me if I would forgive him. "It's not a problem," I said. He retorted, "Listen, you don't understand. I really need you to forgive me. I don't want the junk of prejudice and racism spilling over into my kids' lives. I didn't vote for you, and I was wrong. God is using your preaching to impact my life."

This man heard God and was acting on what he heard. I forgave him. We hugged for a good while, weeping in each other's arms. I was moved and humbled, and I rejoiced in being reminded that God had me in the right place at the right time doing the right thing.

That next Sunday we wrapped up Malachi, and people were invited to share how the series had impacted their lives. The gentleman I had met stood up and told what God had done in his heart. The congregation cheered and whistled, and I sensed that God was on the move creating His Church.[2]

We can grace the doors of our church every Sunday, worship to our heart's content, sit under profound teachings from our servant leaders, all this, and yet remain unaware that by not allowing old aberrant partialities to pass away, we are preventing ourselves from becoming a new creation. This is clearly in opposition to 2 Cor 5:17, which reads, "Therefore, if anyone is in Christ, he is a new creation. The old has passed away; behold, the new has come."

---

2. Williams and Lopus, "True Story."

THE ISSUE

Notwithstanding all we have learned throughout the Gospels regarding how we are to love one another (see John 13:34), to "do to others as you would have them do to you" (Luke 6:31), we have missed the mark. One of the most often used descriptions of the early church is that "all the believers were one in heart and mind" (Acts 4:32). Acts 6, unfortunately, sheds another light. Though the church was young, it had grown to extraordinary numbers; the figure reached an estimated twenty thousand men and women. However, there was a discrepancy that was sure to unravel the unity of the new church. The congregation's Hellenist (Greek-speaking) widows became angered by how the daily food distribution was handled. They were being neglected and passed over. In other words, they were discriminated against, which led to the division of two-social groups in the church, the Hebrews and the Hellenists.

GROUPS

The Hellenists were Greek-speaking Jews who were "dispersed," i.e., residing outside Judea among the gentiles (non-Jews). Whereas the Hebrews who were natives of Judea spoke Hebrew and Aramaic, the Hellenists spoke Greek. The dispersion came by way of numerous Jews leaving Israel for economic and political reasons and in hopes of seeking lucrative land. In most cases, the dispersion was not initially voluntary. Conquering nations had subjugated Israel and had sent the Jewish people into exile. Some returned home after captivity, while others remained in gentile countries.[3]

The Hebraic Jews were adamant about expressing their legitimacy through being reared in the land of the patriarchs, as well as their ability to speak the native tongue of their ancestors. This caused much strife. Their pride led to power and privilege, which in turn instigated resentful feelings from the Hellenist group.

---

3. MacArthur, *Study Bible*, loc. 7922.

DIFFERENCE

One commentary on the book of Acts, edited by Clinton E. Arnold, describes what differentiated the two social groups of believers:

> These "Hellenists" tended to be just as zealous about the temple, the law, and the festivals as any Jew raised in Jerusalem (Saul/Paul is a good case in point). There may have been some cultural differences, however, that further distinguished them from the "Hebrews," such as taste in foods, musical styles, and literature. The "Hebrews," on the other hand, in their efforts not to be tainted by Hellenistic culture, may have been more isolationist and ethnocentric, perhaps going to great lengths to avoid contact with other Jews who did not accept their own outlook and interpretation of purity regulations.[4]

Something to Ponder:
How ironic that two groups of believers in Jesus with different backgrounds were viewed as different, leaving one group—the Hellenists—to be seen as outsiders or a marginalized group. This distinction was an act of racism.

Practical points of interest regarding the Hellenist widows:

- They did not believe they were respected or valued like the Hebraic widows.

- They were being treated differently—and valued differently—because of their ethnicity/culture.

- They felt that they did not count or matter and that their needs and lives were not significant.[5]

4. Arnold, *Acts*, loc. 45.

5. These practical points of interest regarding the Hellenist widows were inspired by Horton, "Voices with Ed Stetzer," and Smith, "Acts 6."

On the other hand, the Hebraic widows did not see the issue. Why? Because they were culturally aligned with the majority of the church leaders.

THE SOLUTION

When faced with injustice or unfair treatment, it is a natural human response to cast blame or seek reprisal rather than seek a genuine approach to a solution that will alleviate any physical or emotional harm that has occurred.

> Luke does not tell us who is to blame for this discriminatory treatment faced by the Greek-speaking Jewish widows. The apostles, however, do not undertake a blame-finding investigation. Instead, they immediately seek a solution to the problem.[6]

Only by first acknowledging the complaint and understanding its legitimacy can one handle such cultural unease. The apostles exercised their wisdom by behaving in an authorized, moral manner, by *walking in line* with God's word: "Therefore, brothers, pick out from among you seven men of good repute, full of the Spirit and of wisdom, whom we will appoint to this duty" (Acts 6:3).

- *Among yourselves*
  Intentionally placing Hellenist (Greek-speaking) men in charge of the food distribution exemplifies diversifying the leadership to correct the situation.

- *Good repute*
  They were to choose those known to be worthy of esteem amongst the Hellenist culture.

- *Full of the Spirit*
  These men needed to not only excel in natural abilities to administrate and lead, but they also needed to demonstrate the presence of the Holy Spirit in their lives.

---

6. Arnold, *Acts*, loc. 2130.

- *Full of wisdom*
  They were to have the ability to apply God's truth appropriately to life situations.[7]

The apostles essentially answered the call for justice and mercy. It was apparent that all widows' lives mattered. They heard the hurting widows and identified with them in their hurt. They corrected an injustice by putting into practice the words of the prophet Micah: "What does the LORD require of you but to do justice, and to love kindness, and to walk humbly with your God?" (Mic 6:8 ESV).

RESPONSE

If Scripture is well-defined in how we are to love one another despite our differences, what would be some reasons that some people would find Scripture's instructions on this difficult to accept?

_____

_____

_____

_____

_____

_____

_____

What are some of the intentional movements your church has made embracing and celebrating the unique differences that other cultures can offer the church?

_____

_____

_____

7. Barton, *Life Application Study Bible*, 490.

_____

_____

_____

_____

What are some specific demographic interests regarding worship music, programs, etc., to which your church caters? How would these specific interests make other ethnicities feel overlooked?

_____

_____

_____

_____

_____

_____

What approach did the apostles take in addressing this dilemma? What steps would you take to correct any biases—whether premeditated or unintentional—in the church?

_____

_____

_____

_____

_____

_____

PRAY

Your kingdom is founded on righteousness and justice;
love and faithfulness are shown in all you do. Lord, I pray
for the confidence to speak up for people who cannot
speak for themselves. Protect the rights of all who are
helpless. I know that kindness shown to the poor is an
act of worship, and if I oppress the poor, I insult you who
made them. You have made known what is right and what
you demand: that we see that justice is done; let mercy be
our first concern, and let us humbly obey you. Amen.

For he himself is our peace, who has made the two groups one and has destroyed the barrier, the dividing wall of hostility, by setting aside in his flesh the law with its commands and regulations. His purpose was to create in himself one new humanity out of the two, thus making peace, and in one body to reconcile both of them to God through the cross, by which he put to death their hostility. He came and preached peace to you who were far away and peace to those who were near. For through him we both have access to the Father by one Spirit. (Eph 2:14–18)

Lesson 3

The Wall of Hostility

It is appalling that the most segregated hour of Christian America is eleven o'clock on Sunday morning, the same hour when many are standing to sing: "In Christ There Is No East Nor West."[1]

THE ROOTS OF SEGREGATION were so ingrained in the fabric of America, that it left an everlasting stain on the way we interact with one another. Though there has been some strides to externally remove the stigma of prejudice we have much more work to do in and outside of the church.

> The interracial etiquette that governed the inter-actions between whites and blacks during the Jim Crow era (c. 1876—1965), made it virtually impossible for a genuine relationship to form between members of the two races. One of the most stringent commandments of the interracial etiquette is that you shall not partake of food with

1. King, *Toward Freedom*, 202, quoted in Eng, "Ethnic-Specific Church."

a person of the other race. Wherever possible you are supposed to sit at separate tables, preferably with some article of furniture between the tables to further symbolize the segregation. Here's how one group lived up to this etiquette under difficult circumstance: Four Southern white fisherman, together with a non-white man whom they had hired to row their boat, found themselves in the middle of a lake at Lunchtime. Before partaking of food, they required the non-white sit in the bow of the boat and laid a fishing pole laterally across the boat to segregate him from them.[2]

An article of furniture, fishing pole, or stone slab are merely some of the lengths to which one would go to put up a metaphorical wall to denote their discomfort with groups of people who do not share their racial identity or heritage. A wall clearly represents aggression, which incites a myriad of emotions—namely fear, an emotion that precipitates separation on both sides of the wall.

THE DIVIDING WALL

The dividing wall has been described in other translations as the middle wall of partition, the barrier, the wall of hostility, or the dividing wall of hostility. It alludes to the first-century Herodian Temple and the partition (or railing) that existed between the Court of the Gentiles and the inner courts accessible by the Jews. As if that were not enough, "the Jewish historian, Josephus, informs us that thirteen stone slabs written in Greek and Latin stood at intervals on the barrier, warning Gentiles not to enter. Archaeologists have discovered two of these tablets. Their inscription reads: 'No foreigner is to enter within the forecourt and the balustrade around the sanctuary. Whoever is caught will have himself to blame for his subsequent death.'"[3]

---

2. Kennedy, *Jim Crow Guide*, 208.
3. Arnold et al., *Ephesians, Philippians*, loc. 1160.

Something to Ponder:
These walls were symbolic of religious, social, and spiritual separation to keep Jews and gentiles apart.

CLOSER LOOK

Metaphorical walls can be found throughout history, including in the United States, where segregation's central purpose was to maintain a second-class status for non-whites while upholding a first-class social and economic status for whites. These legislative "Jim Crow" laws were created with the intent to separate.

However, in the case of Israel, the separation was being used by God to bring forth a divine purpose. The concept of the *wall* takes us back to the law in the Old Testament. God elected Israel to serve as his chosen people, which led to a host of responsibilities including setting up good and healthy boundaries—boundaries guided by numerous laws ranging from moral to dietary laws. This separated them from other nations and exemplified God's holiness. Israel was appointed by God to live as a beacon to the entire world, "a kingdom of priests and a holy nation" (Exod 19:6; 1 Pet 2:9; Rev 1:6), but unchecked biases and privilege can cloud people's judgment and work against God's plan.

These boundaries were for the sake of Israel's unique relationship to God. They were never intended to exist as hostile walls of division but were rather for the preservation of blessing to the world.

THE CROSS

One of the most monumental moments in history is captured in the book of Mark: "And Jesus uttered a loud cry and breathed his last. And the curtain of the temple was torn in two, from top to bottom" (15:37–38). At this instant, God told the world that humanity's relationship with Him and others would never be the same. The veil between the Holy Place and the Most Holy Place that separated humanity and God was removed, tearing down all walls—metaphorical or otherwise. The death of Christ provided the necessary sacrifice for both Jews and non-Jews to access God. Therefore, a new person in Christ is no longer Jew or non-Jew, only Christian.

REFLECTION

The following reflection enlightens us about the severity of Christ's selfless act on the cross and how it impacts us today regarding our admittance to him without any barriers despite our differences:

> Christ has not only overcome the divisions separating Jews from Gentiles, but also every barrier that separates people from one another today. This includes race, social status, denominations, and every other dividing wall that we may choose to erect. Our churches should showcase to the world the unifying power of the gospel. How is your church doing? Do you harbor any pride, bitterness, or animosity toward other believers in your heart? The gospel demands that we work toward unity.[4]

THE REALITY

One of the primary foci of this book is self-examination. For believers to significantly impact the world, it starts with us (the household of faith). We should not only recognize and shed ourselves of biases but also embrace the differences of others. "Therefore welcome one another as Christ has welcomed you, for the glory of God" (Rom 17:7).

> But sadly, Christians often re-erect walls between one another. That is why Paul urges us to "walk worthy of the calling . . . bearing with one another in love, endeavoring to keep the unity of the Spirit in the bond of

---

4. Arnold et al., *Ephesians, Philippians*, loc. 1153.

peace" (4:1–3). Rather than building walls, let's work to dismantle what separates us. Let the world see that we are indeed of the same household.[5]

These associations should be built on genuine relationships, not superficial ones. Often, churches seeking to be multicultural approach ethnic relationships intentionally rather than allowing them to happen organically. The metaphorical wall is intentionality, whether conscious or subconscious; however, once removed, we are naturally compelled to embrace one another's differences to build genuine relationships.

RESPONSE

How would you summarize your assessment of this narrative?

_____

_____

_____

_____

_____

_____

_____

What metaphorical walls have you put up against others?

_____

_____

_____

_____

_____

_____

5. Hia, "Dividing Wall."

What do you believe would be fruitful criticism regarding biases noticed by others?

_____

_____

_____

_____

_____

_____

_____

What steps will you take in tearing down the walls of hostility going forward?

_____

_____

_____

_____

_____

_____

_____

PRAY

> Lord, help me to walk in a manner worth of the calling
> to which you have called me, with all humility and
> gentleness, with patience, bearing with others in love,
> eager to maintain the unity of the Spirit in the bond of
> peace, always recognizing that there is one body and
> one Spirit—one Lord, one faith, one baptism. Amen.

When Cephas came to Antioch, I opposed him to his face, because he stood condemned. For before certain men came from James, he used to eat with the Gentiles. But when they arrived, he began to draw back and separate himself from the Gentiles because he was afraid of those who belonged to the circumcision group. The other Jews joined him in his hypocrisy, so that by their hypocrisy even Barnabas was led astray. When I saw that they were not acting in line with the truth of the gospel, I said to Cephas in front of them all, "You are a Jew, yet you live like a Gentile and not like a Jew. How is it, then, that you force Gentiles to follow Jewish customs?" (Gal 2:11–14)

Lesson 4

Walking in Line with the Gospel

I was convinced that worship at its best is a social experience with people of all levels of life coming together to realize their oneness and unity under God. Whenever the church, consciously or unconsciously, caters to one class it loses the spiritual force of the "whosoever will, let him come" doctrine and is in danger of becoming a little more than a social club with a thin veneer of religiosity.[1]

CONVERSATIONS CAN BE DAUNTING or outright uncomfortable. Nevertheless, they must be entered into so we can learn about one another. An open line of communication can lead to deeper connections, eventually leading to trust. I was intrigued by an interesting story by Lesa Engelthaler regarding her experience that spoke to this very issue:

---

1. AZ Quotes, "Martin Luther King, Jr."

"So you will be my White friend," Rosemary said, and we both started laughing. But we hadn't been laughing before.

I met Rosemary Knight about three years ago when she was new to our church and was interested in going on our women's mission trip to Nicaragua. Our relationship moved into friendship on that trip. I don't remember how the conversation got started, but while taking a break from painting a house, I asked Rosemary if she was uncomfortable at our church. She said yes and I said I didn't blame her. Looking back on the conversation, Rosemary reflected, "That shocked me. She's White, why is she saying that? It was like a brokenness began in you."

After returning home from Nicaragua, Rosemary invited me to her home for breakfast. She said, "I trusted you, so I invited you into my comfort place." Over bacon and eggs, Rosemary told me that even though our church was mostly white, she chose to attend because it was in her neighborhood. She felt she could help us with diversity, but admitted to not realizing how lonely it would feel.

The week following the Dallas shooting last summer, Rosemary, two other Black women and I carpooled to a community prayer meeting. Later, Rosemary asked me if I felt uncomfortable on the drive and I asked her if there was anything I could have done better. It was hard to hear but she challenged me saying, "Lesa, you move too fast too soon with people, it's like you're interviewing them. You need to earn the right to get personal."

I have learned that conversations with people of different races can be uncomfortable. I need grace from my friends, like Rosemary, to let me know when I get it wrong, and then help me to try again.[2]

We all, at times, have been faced with the fear of the unknown: Will I ask the wrong question, or will I say the wrong thing? It is OK to ask questions, to get it wrong, and to enter into uncomfortable conversations. Chances are the person on the receiving end will be more than gracious in answering and offering constructive advice.

---

2. Engelthaler, "Three Stories," paras. 14–18.

In the case of Paul and Peter, regarding the discrepancy at Antioch involving Peter's separation from the gentiles, the following study shows a less-than-authentic relationship that could be injurious to the faith of non-Jews.

One commentator has described the following lesson captured from Gal 2:11–14 as "the darkest of days in the history of the gospel."[3] At first glance, one may conclude that this commentator's description may sound a bit extreme. However, when our actions confuse and hurt other believers, we essentially undermine the gospel message, which can be very destructive.

CERTAIN MEN

The Jerusalem Council (Acts 15) initiated an edict that gentiles did not have to be circumcised. However, Gal 2:12 mentions "certain men" (the legalistic group) claiming to be from James (leader of the Jerusalem church) who were bent on the idea that, for gentiles to be accepted, they must conform or assimilate to their way of worship and practices—that, essentially, they needed to convert to Judaism.

Apparently, this group did not receive the apostles' instructions. Some commentators say they were a part of a legalistic group of the church. Today's churches are filled with many groups with varying ideologies about their faith. Some hold to traditional views, others to a more progressive stance, etc. The legalistic group of Paul's day had a more conventional approach, one that says *to be part of us, you must be like us,* imposing on others the Mosaic law—specifically circumcision and kosher dietary laws. Therefore, if anyone wanted to be part of the church, they would have to essentially relinquish their cultural identity. In other words, acceptance came with the caveat of assimilation.

---

3. MacArthur, *Study Bible,* loc. 297930.

NOT WALKING IN LINE

Peter on occasion had acted faithfully in befriending and eating alongside his gentile brothers and sisters (believers); he was allowed into their comfort space. Peter intentionally went to Antioch to support the gentile church and to learn more about the workings of their outreach to other gentiles in the community.

However, after certain Jewish men whom James had sent came from Jerusalem, Peter gradually withdrew from eating with the gentiles and accompanied his Jewish companions from Jerusalem. According to Ralph P. Martin, "he cut himself off"—a possible pun, meaning "he played the Pharisee." (*Pharisee* is built on a Semitic root meaning "to separate.")[4] Peter was disregarding the previous decision made at the Jerusalem Council regarding the establishment of fellowship between Jewish and gentile Christians (Acts 15:7–14). Many of the resolutions proposed were by Peter himself, much of which he had come to grips with in his own experience of befriending gentiles (10:34–43). James, Jesus's brother, the head of the Jerusalem Council, had endorsed Peter's mission to the gentiles.

We see here a clear example in Peter's actions, which warn us against peer pressure and betraying the trusted relationships one has built with believers from other ethnicities. Often, we can allow certain groups or church members to sway us from following God's word, resulting in the alienation of other groups.

Welcoming different cultures into the fold can cause discomfort in some. Others choose to hold onto their innate biases. Peter's actions undermined the gospel message, and he was not walking in line with God's word.

Something to Ponder:
"The actions of Peter and the rest were a practical denial of the gospel. Paul acted decisively when it became apparent to him that 'they were not straightforward

---

4. Moo et al., *Romans, Galatians*, loc. 4146.

about the truth of the gospel' (v. 14). What Peter did compelled the gentiles to live like Jews (v. 14), which was, in Paul's words, 'another gospel' (cf. 1:6–7)."[5]

THE OPPOSITION

A face-to-face confrontation ensued between two prominent leaders of the faith—Paul and Peter. Peter's inappropriate behavior toward the non-Jews (gentiles) struck a chord with Paul. Peter, however, was not alone in this hypocritical behavior toward the gentiles. Other Jews, including Barnabas, followed suit. Barnabas's name being singled out among the other Jews by Paul may indicate a shock or disappointment in his traveling companion's action (Gal 2:13). Paul's rebuke of Peter's behavior was as public as Peter's action; he dealt with this injustice in earshot of all who stood accused. The gentile believers had allowed Peter into their comfort space because they trusted him. He accepted them for who they were, not trying to assimilate them into another culture but into faith in Christ. Peter's authority as an apostle thus deepened whatever confusion or speculation may have existed among the gentile believers regarding love and unity between Jews and gentiles. Because Peter's sin was public, Paul needed to correct Peter publicly to salvage what damage had been caused by his actions with the gentile believers. Ginetta Sagan, an Italian-born American human rights activist, has a quote that embodies the action of the Apostle Paul: "Silence in the face of injustice is complicity with the oppressor."[6]

---

5. Deffinbaugh, "Peter's Capitulation," para. 22.

6. Joffe, "Ginetta Sagan," para. 10.

WALKING IN LINE

Over a hundred verses in the Bible, directly and indirectly, command us to love our neighbor. Jesus could have been no more explicit than in Mark 12:30–31 when he issues the edict, "Love the Lord your God with all your heart and with all your soul and with all your mind and with all your strength," adding, "You shall love your neighbor as yourself." He concludes, "There is no other commandment greater than these."

Remarkably, both these commands share the same character—genuine love for God evidenced by a genuine love for people. One time, a scribe (an expert of the law) asked Jesus, "And who is my neighbor?" (Luke 10:29). Jesus replied by telling him the story of the good Samaritan. This story highlights that a neighbor is not someone you know personally or a person of your own culture or ethnicity (see lesson 5). We are called not only to love those like us or those with whom we feel comfortable but all those individuals God places in our path.[7]

Walking in line with the gospel is essential for a genuine follower of Christ. Love supplants our formerly held beliefs and biases. An internal change must take place in order to walk in line, a change that Christ is willing to help you make. In the book of Ezekiel, God made a promise to Israel, a promise that permeates the hearts of believers today. For us to accomplish or follow his precepts, his Spirit has to enable us to do so: "I will give you a new heart and put a new spirit in you; I will remove from you your heart of stone and give you a heart of flesh. And I will put my Spirit in you and move you to follow my decrees and be careful to keep my laws" (Ezek 36:26–27).

The question then is, Are you willing to change? Do you want to become a new creature? Not accepting all of God's children is not walking in line with the gospel. Jesus's own words confirm this truth: "Just as I have loved you, you also are to love one another. By this all people will know that you are my disciples, if you have love for one another" (John 13:34–35).

7. Got Questions, "Who Is My Neighbor?"

RESPONSE

What are some of the peer pressures you have experienced that have caused you to withhold evangelizing efforts toward people of other cultures?

_____

_____

_____

_____

_____

_____

_____

As a church leader or member of a particular church, what are some of the conscience or unconscious efforts of the church that you have seen to find ways to assimilate other cultures into their idea or brand of a church?

_____

_____

_____

_____

_____

_____

_____

How would you respond to those who feel uncomfortable with other cultures or groups being part of their church?

_____

_____

_____

_____

_____

_____

_____

How does embracing bias and discrimination reflect a different gospel?

_____

_____

_____

_____

_____

_____

_____

PRAY

May God grant me the ability to walk in step with the gospel, and may God give me the kind of genuine love for others that motivates personal realignment. Let me come near with a sincere heart in full assurance that faith provides. In Jesus's name, I pray. Amen.

And behold, a lawyer stood up to put him to the test, saying, "Teacher, what shall I do to inherit eternal life?"

He said to him, "What is written in the law? How do you read it?"

And he answered, "You shall love the Lord your God with all your heart and with all your soul and with all your strength and with all your mind, and your neighbor as yourself."

And he said to him, "You have answered correctly; do this, and you will live."

But he, desiring to justify himself, said to Jesus, "And who is my neighbor?"

Jesus replied, "A man was going down from Jerusalem to Jericho, and he fell among robbers, who stripped him and beat him and departed, leaving him half dead. Now by chance a priest was going down that road, and when he saw him he passed by on the other side.

So likewise a Levite, when he came to the place and saw him, passed by on the other side.

But a Samaritan, as he journeyed, came to where he was, and when he saw him, he had compassion. He went to him and bound up his wounds, pouring on oil and wine. Then he set him on his own animal and brought him to an inn and took care of him. And the next day he took out two denarii and gave them to the innkeeper, saying, 'Take care of him, and whatever more you spend, I will repay you when I come back.' Which of these three, do you think, proved to be a neighbor to the man who fell among the robbers?" He said, "The one who showed him mercy."

And Jesus said to him, "You go, and do likewise." (Luke 10:25–37)

Lesson 5

Who Is My Neighbor?

Justice goes across racial and economic
barriers—like the good Samaritan.[1]

THE POLICE SUBCULTURE HAS been vilified to no end. That is not
to say there have not been some unfortunate misdeeds by some in
their ranks. However, the few should not outweigh the many. Of-
tentimes, the pain felt by those on the receiving end of someone's
indignation leaves an indelible scar and, with it, a perception of that
individual or group that would be hard to erase from the psyche.

Biblically, we must all forgive, especially when it's hard. For-
giving others in whatever capacity unveils why God's mercy is in-
fallible to the world around us. An often-quoted statement among
believers still rings true today, "You may be the only Bible some
people ever read. So the question is: Are you a good translator?"[2]

1. Perkins, "162 Racial Equality Quotes," para. 31.
2. Batterson, "Quotes."

I read an intriguing story about the George Floyd protests. The story teaches us that the idea of painting a group of people with a broad brush can rob us of the opportunity of recognizing individual efforts of kindness and compassion within a larger group.

Simeon Bartee, along with his wife and their five-year-old daughter, observed a demonstration in downtown Houston. Numerous police officers were patrolling the area. Bartee's daughter became frightened by the presence of the officers and asked her father, "Are they going to shoot us?"[3]

In a reassuring gesture, an officer knelt in front of Simeon's daughter and told her that they were there to protect her and not to harm anyone. Bartee said his daughter asked, "Can we protest?"[4]

The officer responded, "You can protest, you can march, you can do whatever you want—just don't break nothing."[5]

The tensions between the police and the Black community were particularly high at that time, especially after the death of George Floyd at the hands of a police officer, which highlighted the need for reform in law enforcement practices. Bartee shared that his brother was brutally beaten by police officers in 2016 and needed reconstructive surgery due to his injuries.

The officer's concern and kindness towards Bartee's daughter left a lasting impression on him. "I just want to thank the officer for giving me a different perspective on what police officers, the good police officers, are like."[6]

Bartee told the reporter "he believes his daughter also received a new perspective after speaking with the officer. He said the officer later told Simone that he had a daughter and he wanted to make it home for his daughter, too." Bartee said, "She looked up at me and said, 'I didn't know police officers had kids.'"[7]

The consolatory efforts of someone we may deem the enemy could be alarming at first. However, in moments of distress,

---

3. Sanz, "Officer Comforts Girl," para. 2.

4. Sanz, "Officer Comforts Girl," para. 4.

5. Sanz, "Officer Comforts Girl," para. 5.

6. Sanz, "Officer Comforts Girl," para. 7.

7. Sanz, "Officer Comforts Girl," para. 9.

comfort is welcome despite how it's packaged. A tender voice or a helping hand can cause anyone to rethink former perceptions of a person or group.

The primary focus of this lesson will be on the curious lawyer and the merciful Samaritan. The crux of the message is centered on how those who profess to know and hold fast to God's word can often have a very partial view of Scripture related to who their neighbor is.

THE LAWYER

The scribes were neither a religious sect nor a political party but a professional class. "Lawyer, scribe, and teacher (of the law) are synonymous terms in the New Testament. Scribes interpreted and taught the Old Testament law and delivered legal pronouncements on cases brought to them."[8] Not only was it their business to study the law, but they would also transcribe it and write commentaries. However, on the other hand, they would intermingle manufactured traditions with God's law, and over time those traditions began to eclipse God's law. Much of the following dialogue between the lawyer and Jesus confirms this idea.

The lawyer begins with a pertinent question, a question asked by others throughout the Gospels (Matt 19:16–22; John 3:1–15), "Teacher[,] . . . what must I do to inherit eternal life?" (Luke 10:25). Jesus, knowing the lawyer's presumed expertise, asks him, "What is written in the law? How do you read it?" (v. 26).

Jesus's tactic of answering a question with a question (as he does here) is referred to as the Socratic method. The lawyer answers by quoting Deut 6:5 and Lev 19:18, "Love the Lord your God with all your heart and with all your soul and with all your strength and with all your mind, and your neighbor as yourself" (Luke 10:27). After Jesus accepts his answer, the lawyer exposes his sanctimonious character by asking, "And who is my neighbor?" (v. 29). This is an improper question because the lawyer is trying to exclude responsibility for others by making some people not

8. Gundry, *Survey of the New Testament*, loc. 1626–29.

neighbors. A more appropriate question would have been, "How can I be a loving neighbor?"[9]

Some of the Jewish experts in the Law embraced a somewhat biased view of *neighbor*. We have learned throughout the lessons that they had little to no contact with gentiles, Hellenistic Jews, or those who were not learners of the Mosaic law, which left only one sort of person worthy of being considered a neighbor: those very much like themselves.

If we are not careful, we too can take a similar approach to the term neighbor. Excluding those who do not hold to our standards and principles and leaving only those who are like us leads to homogeneous churches and communities. Although there may be a semblance of diversity in some cases, it could simply be assimilation.

> "Xenophobia and racial prejudice have always been a great divider among nations. Since the ancient times to the present, we tend to distrust others who don't look like us or sound like us."[10]

THE SAMARITAN

So, who is my neighbor? Jesus answers this question by telling the man a story (Luke 10:30–37), illustrating a familiar occurrence to the listeners. A man was traveling from Jerusalem to Jericho, an eighteen-mile stretch of road over a winding, rocky terrain, with a descent of 3,200 feet,[11] that was also a prime opportunity for robbers. The traveler in this story had fallen victim to thieves and was beaten to within an inch of his life.

He was overlooked by two passersby: a priest whose task was to perform the duties in the temple of Jerusalem and a Levite

9. MacArthur, *Study Bible*, loc. 8470.

10. Ponio, "Good Samaritan Story," para. 13.

11. MacArthur, *Study Bible*, loc. 8470.

whose responsibility was to assist the priest in his duties. At face value, these were the likely men to care for this victim, but the unimaginable happens when instead a Samaritan renders care and support for this man. The Samaritan was risking his life in this crime-ridden area, not to mention the aggression of other travelers due to his cultural difference.

Many Jews in this time harbored a deep disdain for Samaritans because they were a product of the intermarriage between Jews and gentiles. The religious stance of the Samaritans also played a part in this hatred. The Jews embraced the first five books of the Hebrew Bible (the Law) as well as the books of poetry and prophecy. The Samaritans, however, only recognized the first five books of the Law. The Jews had no dealings with them and considered them the vilest of humans. Both Jews and Samaritans would go out of their way to avoid contact, including taking longer travel routes. So, one can see how this story could gnaw at the heart of a Jewish hearer.

Nevertheless, the Samaritan did not consider the stranger's race or religion. The care unveiled in this story is a level of care that would be more than sufficient for a stranger, let alone a rival. The Samaritan tended to the man's wounds, placed him on his animal, took him to an inn, continued to care for him, and gave the innkeeper a generous amount of money (two *denarii*, two days' wages) to continue the care, promising to return if there were any additional costs.

I believe the lack of mention of the victim's name and race was as consequential to the story as the man's name and race was inconsequential to the Samaritan. He simply saw a neighbor in dire need of assistance.

Something to Ponder:

"The first question which the priest and the Levite asked was: 'If I stop to help this man, what will happen to me?' But . . . the good Samaritan reversed the question: 'If I don't stop to help this man, what will happen to him?'"[12]

---

12. King, quoted in Conner, "King on Complacency," para. 10.

WALKING IN LINE

Jesus then asked the lawyer a rather common-sense question, "Which of these three, do you think, proved to be a neighbor to the man who fell among the robbers?" (Luke 10:36). The lawyer gives the correct answer: "The one who showed him mercy" (v. 37). Though his answer was right, his heart reflected some hostility that kept him from saying "the Samaritan." Instead, he referred to him as "the one who . . ."

This lesson mirrors the recurring theme that runs through those that preceded it. Despite one's race or religion, we are to show love and compassion toward everyone. This should also be seen in our generosity and giving. A plethora of Scriptures testify to the enmity between these two groups. However, whenever racial or biased divisions intersect with the gospel, they are often met with opposition. "It is not the person from the radically different culture on the other side of the world who is hardest to love but the nearby neighbor whose skin color, language, rituals, values, ancestry, history, and customs are different from one's own."[13] Jesus clearly broke down Jewish and Samaritan barriers when he shared the gospel with the Samaritan woman in John 4:1–26. The apostle Phillip advanced this campaign in the city of Samaria in Acts 8:25. Do you agree that we should continue this movement?

"YOU GO AND DO LIKEWISE"

Jesus ends this dialogue with a defining instruction, "You go, and do likewise." Love is, after all, action and should not be restricted by the object. Though there may be some sacrifice on our part, remember, someone much greater made a sacrifice on our behalf.

REFLECTION

Far too often, we judge others based on their identity. When we encounter someone different from ourselves or outside our comfort

13. Bible.org, "Jews and Samaritans," para. 6.

zone, our instinct is often to avoid or disregard them. As a result, we consciously or unconsciously define who our neighbor is.

> Loving God and loving your neighbor are the two greatest commandments. But who is your neighbor? When Jesus was asked this question, he told a story that shocked his hearers. A true neighbor is one who is willing to look past the differences that traditionally divide people and to love others unconditionally and without prejudice. Who would God have you to reach out to today?[14]

RESPONSE

Before hearing the story of the good Samaritan, who or what did you consider a *neighbor* to be?

_____

_____

_____

_____

_____

_____

Which character in this story do you identify with the most, and why?

_____

_____

_____

_____

_____

_____

14. Strauss, "Good Samaritan," 270.

What are some personal sacrifices you can make to help others regardless of their race or belief system?

_____

_____

_____

_____

_____

_____

How will you follow Jesus's challenge to *go and do likewise*?

_____

_____

_____

_____

_____

_____

PRAY

Lord, we love because you first loved us. By truthfully loving you, I must not hate my neighbor; I would be a liar by doing so. Help me to love as you have earnestly loved me. Forgive me of any offenses or strife I may have stirred up in the past or present. I know love covers all offenses, and those who love you must love their neighbor.

Large crowds were traveling with Jesus, and turning to them he said: "If anyone comes to me and does not hate father and mother, wife and children, brothers and sisters—yes, even their own life—such a person cannot be my disciple. And whoever does not carry their cross and follow me cannot be my disciple."

"Suppose one of you wants to build a tower. Won't you first sit down and estimate the cost to see if you have enough money to complete it? For if you lay the foundation and are not able to finish it, everyone who sees it will ridicule you, saying, 'This person began to build and wasn't able to finish.'

"Or suppose a king is about to go to war against another king. Won't he first sit down and consider whether he is able with ten thousand men to oppose the one coming against him with twenty thousand? If he is not able, he will send a delegation while the other is still a long way off and will ask for terms of peace. In the same way, those of you who do not give up everything you have cannot be my disciples.

"Salt is good, but if it loses its saltiness, how can it be made salty again? It is fit neither for the soil nor for the manure pile; it is thrown out. Whoever has ears to hear, let them hear." (Luke 14:25–34)

Lesson 6

The Cost

Salvation is free, but discipleship costs everything we have.[1]

On November 8, 1961, Dr. Martin Luther King Jr. (1929–68), the great civil rights leader, arrived for his only visit to Seattle.... Reverend Samuel B. McKinney had invited him to be part of a lecture series sponsored by the Brotherhood of Mount Zion Baptist Church. McKinney was pastor of the church and a friend and had been a classmate of King at Morehouse College in Atlanta.

Arrangements were made for Dr. King to speak at First Presbyterian Church because Mount Zion would not be large enough to handle the numbers expected. First Presbyterian Church canceled the oral agreement to rent the sanctuary to Mount Zion just weeks before King's scheduled arrival and shortly after advertisements of his lecture were already circulated. The reasons ranged from construction work to other commitments, but McKinney attributed it to racism. He appealed to First

1. Graham, "Marks of Christ?," para. 14.

Presbyterian church leaders, but this produced other excuses, such as the use of the sanctuary [was] only for religious meetings and the reluctance to have proceeds go not to Mount Zion's building fund but to King's enterprises. Local organizations and churches denounced the cancellation. The Christian Friends for Racial Equality, Grace Methodist Church, the Baptist Ministers Conference of Seattle and Vicinity, and the Capitol Hill Ministerial Association voiced shock and disapproval. Even the Presbytery of Seattle commended King to its member churches.

Other venues were offered immediately. King arrived the evening of November 8 and checked into the Olympic Hotel. He gave his first lecture at the University of Washington on Thursday, November 9, in the old Meany Hall, before 2,000 students. They gave him a standing ovation. That evening he spoke at Temple de Hirsch. On November 10, he spoke at Garfield High School and that evening at the Eagles Auditorium (now ACT Theatre). A reception followed at Plymouth Congregational Church.[2]

> "'I saw a note from First Presbyterian church— typed, generated by a machine,' McKinney said in a videotaped interview. 'It was an apology for what had happened. I got him on the phone. He came to the church. I said I never expected this to happen. . .'"[3]

FOLLOWING CHRIST IS COSTLY

This turn of events was on the heels of Jim Crow,[4] though many felt that Jim Crow laws were only prevalent in the South. The North

2. Henry, "Martin Luther King Jr. Arrives," paras. 1–3.
3. Raftery, "King Workshopped Speech in Seattle," para. 30.
4. See Glossary, s.v. "Wall of Hostility."

was not immune to Jim-Crow-like laws. Schools and neighbor-hoods were segregated, and voting rights were designed to make it nearly impossible for Blacks to vote.[5] Signs displaying "White Only" were still being placed in the windows of local businesses.

Could there be a reason to believe during the heightened vis-ibility of the Civil Rights Movement that a pastor and civil rights leader coming to speak in the pulpit of a predominately white church would cause a decline in congregants or affect their bottom line? Perhaps so. Though First Presbyterian had rescinded their invitation, King went on to workshop his iconic "I Have a Dream" speech at these other three Seattle locations.

This study is not designed to cast shame on any institution or conjure up old wounds but merely to examine the cost of following Christ in crucial times. Years later, as Rev. McKinney explains, the First Presbyterian Church apologized for rescinding the invitation.

The justice of God can be defined as "that essential and in-finite attribute which makes his nature and his ways the perfect embodiment of equity, and constitutes him [as] the model and the guardian of equity throughout the universe."[6] This is seen through-out Scripture and exemplified in his mercifulness. Psalm 82:3–4 states, "Defend the weak and the fatherless; uphold the cause of the poor and the oppressed. Rescue the weak and the needy; deliver them from the hand of the wicked." We, as believers, have been deputized with the charge of being God's ambassadors on earth with the task of protecting the marginalized and oppressed.

The Gospel of Luke recounts the words of Jesus on the terms of discipleship (Luke 14:25–34). These verses uniquely depict what it means to follow Christ and the losses that may occur in many areas, including our relationships, dreams, possessions, and, most importantly, our very lives. So why is this cost so high, and why must it be counted?

Often on the road of faith and in the world, we will be faced with making sacrifices at the intersection of allegiance to Christ

---

5. Some states required Black people to own property before they could vote.

6. Rand, "Justice," para. 2.

and capitulation to culture. One who has not carefully counted the cost will turn away from the road of faith, veering so effortlessly toward the world and turning away at the risk of sacrifice. First John 2:15 gives a stark reminder to those who choose the world: "Do not love the world or anything in the world." The word love here denotes affection and devotion, which belong first to God. The world is a spiritual system influenced by Satan and opposed to God and his word. So, for one to allow the world to supersede God's word in how we interact with others, according to 1 John 2:15, "the Father is not in them." Therefore, we must renounce all, hate all,[7] in order to become his disciple. Our love for "Father and mother, wife and children, brothers and sisters—even our very lives" (Luke 14:25) should not overtake our love for Christ.

This means that to deny justice is equivalent to saying, I renounce the directives and principles of the Lord and instead submit to the ideas of the world. Following Christ will be costly to some.

> "The life of discipleship can only be maintained as long as nothing is allowed to come between Christ and ourselves, neither the law, nor personal piety, nor even the world. The disciple always looks only to his [or her] master, never to Christ *and* the law, Christ *and* religion, Christ *and* the world. Only by following Christ alone can he [or she] preserve a single eye."[8]

COUNTING THE COST

William Samuelson and Richard Zeckhauser introduced the term *status quo bias* in 1988. As Cynthia Vinney describes,

---

7. The *hatred* called for here is to hold as a lesser love.
8. Bonhoeffer, *Cost of Discipleship*, 173 (emphasis mine).

Status quo bias refers to the phenomenon of preferring that one's environment and situation remain as they already are. The phenomenon is most impactful in the realm of decision-making: when we make decisions, we tend to prefer the more familiar choice over the less familiar.[9]

Though status quo bias affects our behavior and impacts many of our decisions in the world, as believers, we are held to different practices regarding how we conduct kingdom business.

Throughout the previous lessons, we have evaluated the dos and don'ts of how to move toward a more diverse church community. We have learned how to create more organic relationships and how to embrace the uniqueness of others; most importantly, we've learned how to start from within our heart, which embodies our emotions, will, intellect, and desires.

Status quo bias has numerous psychological principles to glean from. However, one principle speaks to a dilemma that many church leaders face: loss aversion. Samuelson and Zeckhauser's studies have shown that

> when individuals make decisions, they weigh the potential for loss more heavily than the potential for gain. Thus, when looking at a set of choices, they focus more on what they could lose by abandoning the status quo than on what they could gain by trying something new.[10]

As a nonprofit organization, the church's finances are reaped through donations and monetary giving, which Scripture clearly validates. The finances are used for various church matters, mortgages, salaries, missions, and programs. Depending on the location, status of the congregants, and congregation size, some churches prosper more than others, leading to more extensive facilities, more numerous staffing positions, and amenities, which in turn require a substantial budget. Therefore, change for some church leaders will take on a new meaning—risk.

9. Vinney, "Status Quo Bias," para. 1.
10. Vinney, "Status Quo Bias," para. 13.

Thus, the hope of pursuing a more culturally diverse congregation can result in the matter of counting the cost. Several factors may affect the church's bottom line, including newer members with lower household incomes or church members unwilling to share in the vision of multiculturalism, which could result in an exodus of members with a history of substantial giving. Despite expenses, people should always be looked at as souls rather than commodities. We should never forget that it is not money that cares for our needs—it is God.

> "No one can serve two masters. Either you will
> hate the one and love the other, or you will be
> devoted to the one and despise the other. You
> cannot serve both God and money" (Matt 6:24).

DISCIPLESHIP AND COST

The sure mark of being a disciple of Christ is our love for one another, as stated in John 13:35. "By this everyone will know that you are my disciples, if you love one another." In the verse that precedes it, Jesus expresses a new commandment, which he exhibited in his love toward us on the cross. "A new command I give you: Love one another. As I have loved you, so you must love one another" (John 13:34). If the world sees partiality, prejudice, and disagreement between followers of Christ, then that signals a distorted view of Jesus. It leads unbelievers to ask, What does this say about Jesus's love toward me? Is he biased? Does he indulge in petty bickering and division?

> Love is an action that should be evident in our daily lives,
> not a catchphrase. In other words, how can we love others as Jesus loves us? By helping when it's inconvenient,
> giving when it hurts, devoting energy to others' welfare
> rather than our own, and absorbing hurts from others

48

without complaining or fighting back. This kind of love is hard to do, but that is why people notice when you do it.[11]

Cost should never be a factor when it comes to love.

RESPONSE

What were some of the costs that you counted before becoming a believer, and how did those costs impact your life?

_____

_____

_____

_____

_____

_____

What would be some reasons why you would prefer your local church environment to stay the same?

_____

_____

_____

_____

_____

_____

Have you been or are you now part of an assembly that weighs its decisions on the potential for loss more heavily than the potential for gain?

11. Barton et al., *Life Application Study Bible*, loc. 172107–9.

_____

_____

_____

_____

_____

_____

_____

What are some preconceived barriers or justifications for not loving others based upon their ethnicity and/or socioeconomic class status?

_____

_____

_____

_____

_____

_____

_____

PRAY

Father, I ask you to forgive me for tolerating prejudice
in the household of faith. Please set me free from the
influence of public opinion so I may live out my glorious
Christ-originated faith. Thank you for revealing that we
are one body, redeemed by the blood of the Lamb. We are
baptized into Christ and have put on the family likeness
of Christ. We are one in the bonds of love. You are the
God and Father of us all in the name of Jesus. Amen.

After this I looked, and there before me was a great multitude that no one could count, from every nation, tribe, people, and language, standing before the throne and before the Lamb. They were wearing white robes and were holding palm branches in their hands. And they cried out in a loud voice,

> "Salvation belongs to our God,
> who sits on the throne,
> and to the Lamb!"

And all the angels were standing around the throne and around the elders and the four living creatures. They fell down on their faces before the throne and worshiped God, saying,

> "Amen!
> Praise and glory
> and wisdom and thanks and honor
> and power and strength
> be to our God forever and ever.
> Amen!" (Rev 7:9–12)

Lesson 7

The End Result

Prejudice is a burden that confuses the past, threatens the future, and renders the present inaccessible.[1]

SLAVES DEVISED SEVERAL TECHNIQUES to avoid detection of their meetings. One practice was to meet in secluded places—woods, gullies, ravines, and thickets (aptly called "hush harbors"). Kalvin Woods remembered preaching to other slaves and singing and praying while huddled behind quilts and rags, which had been thoroughly wetted, "to keep the sound of their voices from penetrating the air," and then hung up "in the form of a little room" or tabernacle.[2] On one Louisiana plantation, "the slaves would steal away into the woods at night and hold services." They

> would form a circle on their knees around the speaker who would also be on his knees. He would bend forward and speak into or over a vessel of water to drown

1. Maya Angelou, quoted in Kaur, "Big Deal?," para. 1.
2. Raboteau, *Slave Religion*, 215–16.

the sound. If anyone became animated and cried out, the others would quickly stop the noise by placing their hands over the offender's mouth.[3]

When slaves got "happy an' shout[ed]" in their cabins, "couldn't nobody hyar 'em," according to George Young, "'caze dey didn't make no fuss on de dirt flo,'" but just in case, "one stan' in de do' an' watch."[4] The most common device for preserving secrecy was an iron pot or kettle turned upside down to catch the sound. The pot was usually placed in the middle of the cabin floor or at the doorstep, then slightly propped up to hold the sound of the praying and singing from escaping. A variation was to pray or sing softly "with heads together around" the "kettle to deaden the sound."[5] Clara Young recalled, "When dark come, de men folks would hang up a wash pot, bottom upwards, in de little brush church house us had, so's it would catch de noise and de overseer wouldn't hear us singin' and shoutin."[6] According to one account, slaves used the overturned pot to cover the sound of more worldly amusements too: "They would have dances sometimes and turn a pot upside down right in front of the door. They said that would keep the sound from going outside."[7] The previous narrative gives us a harsh reality of enslaved African Americans being grief-stricken with fear if found worshipping the Lord. Singing or praying at home was not permitted, and if found doing so, they were flogged by their master for fear they may be praying against them. An even harsher reality is that there are still countries in the world where Christians are still being tormented and, in most cases, martyred for worshiping God.[8]

3. Raboteau, *Slave Religion*, 215–16.

4. Raboteau, *Slave Religion*, 215–16.

5. Raboteau, *Slave Religion*, 215–16.

6. Raboteau, *Slave Religion*, 215–16.

7. Raboteau, *Slave Religion*, 215–16.

8. "During the World Watch List 2019 reporting period, in the top 50 countries, a total of 1,266 churches or Christian buildings were attacked; 2,635 Christians were detained without trial, arrested, sentenced, and imprisoned; and 4,136 Christians were killed for faith-related reasons. On average, that's 11 Christians killed every day for their faith." Carter, "Most Dangerous," para. 3.

DISTINCTIVENESS

Not allowing one to worship the Lord expressively is counterintuitive and an affront to the gospel, but there is a glorious hope, a joyful expectation! Jesus's message to the apostle John on the island of Patmos is one of unprecedented redemption. The days of stealing away in the night and huddling together in a clandestine service in a dark room will be over. Those atrocities committed years ago will be met with the eternal glory once hoped for and now made a reality.

Revelation 7:9–12 depicts many of God's people from every nation and tribe crying out in their dialect. This illustrates a reality that some church leaders earnestly seek and fervently pray to replicate in their churches today. So why can we not bring a diversity of believers into the church without suppressing their individuality regarding worship?

So far, we have found that fear, prejudice, ignorance, and cost are the malefactors. All other answers to this quandary are left to you, the individual. Assimilation is a form of control and has a psychological effect on culture. The primary focus of this lesson is *distinctiveness*. Note that the previous passage (Rev 7:9–12) in no way insinuates that one is forced or obligated to assimilate to the surrounding culture's linguistics or form of worship. Chances are there were many personalities, and many communicating nonverbally through conscious gestures and movements. Some may view cultural interaction or the joining of two cultures as positive and some, as negative. However, we must consider two words, similar in some ways but different in others—acculturation and assimilation. "Acculturation is the transfer of values and customs from one group to another, while Assimilation [*sic*] is *the cultural absorption of a minority group into the main cultural body*."[9] Acculturation can be interactive in nature—the sharing on the part of a minority group of their culture and traditions with a larger community, with care not to lose the distinctiveness of their cultural values. Whereas, typically, when the minority group is absorbed or assimilated

9. Pediaa, "Assimilation and Acculturation," para. 1 (emphasis mine).

into a larger community, their identity, culture, and traditions are lost. "Assimilation can be a quick process or a gradual change. When a person from the minority group is indistinguishable from others, it is called Full Assimilation [*sic*]. Assimilation could be spontaneous or forced."[10]

A great example of an exchange of acculturation between two differing groups is found in the following excerpt. In the book *Generous Justice: How God's Grace Makes Us Just*, Timothy Keller shares an experience that he and his wife had with an African American student he met while attending seminary. He describes the experience as a "bare-knuckled mentoring about the realities of injustice in American culture."[11]

> "You're a racist, you know," he once said at our kitchen table. "Oh, you don't mean to be, and you don't want to be, but you are. You can't really help it." He said, for example, "When black people do things in a certain way, you say, 'Well, that's your culture.' But when white people do things in a certain way, you say, 'That's just the right way to do things.' You don't realize you really have a culture. You are blind to how many of your beliefs and practices are cultural." We began to see how, in so many ways, we made our cultural biases into moral principles and then judged people of other races as being inferior. His case was so strong and fair that, to our surprise, we agreed with him.[12]

So, for all intents and purposes, the right way is the white way. The Black American gentleman sustained his cultural identity while expressing his awareness of the nascent stages of assimilation. The Western standard of living has permeated its influence throughout the centuries so that when faced with cultural differences, these cultural differences are often met with indifference.

---

10. Pediaa, "Assimilation and Acculturation," para. 10.

11. Keller, *Generous Justice*, 172.

12. Keller, *Generous Justice*, 172.

As awkward as these types of conversations may feel to us, they are to be had and received within the context of the participating parties.

I hope and pray that we can all praise God while celebrating the distinctiveness of those praising alongside us.

> I see the world church as the gathering together of a great symphony orchestra where we don't make every new person coming in play a violin in order to fit in with the rest. We invite the people to come in to play the same score—the Word of God—but to play their own instruments, and in this way there will issue forth a heavenly sound that will grow in the splendor and glory of God as each new instrument is added.[13]

MULTICULTURALISM

In his article, "What is Multiculturalism? Definitions, Theories, and Examples," Robert Longley notes that

> In sociology, multiculturalism describes how a given society deals with cultural diversity. Multiculturalism assumes members of different cultures can coexist peacefully and society is enriched by preserving, respecting, and encouraging cultural diversity.[14]

However, much like acculturation and assimilation, multiculturalism can also have its set of challenges. Though some proponents of multiculturalism acknowledge that people should make a concerted effort to retain or hold on to their culture, some see it as an affront to the predominant culture; there is a perceived fear that it may disrupt social order and threaten its individuality. Longley provides a brief synopsis of two multiculturalism theories:

- *The Melting Pot Theory*: "The melting pot theory of multiculturalism assumes that various immigrant groups will tend

13. Ralph Winter, quoted in Balentine, "Biblical Unity."
14. Longley, "What Is Multiculturalism?," para. 1.

to 'melt together,' abandoning their individual cultures and eventually becoming fully assimilated into the predominant society."[15]

- *The Salad Bowl Theory*: "A more liberal theory of multicultur-alism than the melting pot, the salad bowl theory describes a heterogeneous society in which people coexist but retain at least some of the unique characteristics of their traditional culture."[16]

As believers in the body of Christ (the church), we will likely side with the salad bowl theory. We are not to propose that anyone relinquish their culture, traditions, or identity. Do we relinquish? If we carefully consider the wording in the salad bowl theory, "at least some" characteristics of one's culture and traditions are retained. But who determines what is kept and not kept, and at what point does one feel that someone else's culture is infringing on their way of life?

Longley states, "On the negative side, the cultural differences encouraged by the salad bowl model can divide a society result-ing in prejudice and discrimination."[17] In the previous dialogue between Keller and a Black American, Keller perceived something as not being the "right way to do something" because it did not align with his way of life or culture. It was assumed that the Black American culture was doing it wrong. This essentially says, "My culture is right, and yours is wrong."

However, the beauty of the dialogue between the two is that it was informative, healthy, and aided in potential growth. Often our beliefs and values are ingrained in a system of inherited origins. In *The Idea of Culture*, Terry Eagleton defines culture as "the complex of values, customs, beliefs, and practices which constitute the way of life of a specific group."[18] Subconsciously, we can express a bi-ased approach to multiculturalism if we are not careful.

15. Longley, "What Is Multiculturalism?," para. 8.
16. Longley, "What Is Multiculturalism?," para. 10.
17. Longley, "What Is Multiculturalism?," para. 12.
18. Eagleton, *Idea of Culture*, 34.

"Diversity may be the hardest thing for a society
to live with, and perhaps the most dangerous
thing for a society to be without."[19]

THE END RESULT

Ultimately, multiculturalism is necessary for the church and for humankind as a whole. In Ben Clements's article "Three Benefits of Fostering a Multicultural Church," he writes,

> A first benefit of churches embracing multicultural identities is theological. A multicultural church is a clear outworking of obedience to God's word and will, and follows the pattern set by Christ and the Apostles (Matthew 28:19; Acts 2:5–11; 1 Corinthians 9:20–23; Galatians 3:26–29).[20]

Rebecca McLaughlin rightly affirms that "the Christian movement was multicultural and multiethnic from the outset . . . [and that] Christianity is the most ethnically, culturally, socioeconomically, and racially diverse belief system in all of history."[21] This theme is also evident eschatologically, as Rev 7:9 envisages a vividly multicultural, eternal kingdom. And so, it is not accurate to suggest that the church *should* be multicultural; rather, the church *is* multicultural.

"Any racial reconciliation we've had in this country
has come not out of confrontation but out of a spirit
of reconciliation. If we continue to practice an eye for
an eye and a tooth for a tooth, we'll eventually end up
with a land of people who are blind and toothless."[22]

---

19. William Sloane Coffin Jr., quoted in Pisters, "Reflections," para. 1.
20. Clements, "Three Benefits," para. 6.
21. McLaughlin, *Confronting Christianity*, 35–37.
22. AZ Quotes, "Andrew Young Quotes," para. 4.

RESPONSE

What are some cultural biases you have made into moral principles that you expect other cultures to abide by?

_____

_____

_____

_____

_____

_____

What would be some reasons why people from different cultures should make a concerted effort to retain or hold on to their traditions?

_____

_____

_____

_____

_____

_____

In your own words, explain the melting pot and salad bowl theories.

_____

_____

_____

_____

_____

_____

_____

How has this particular study reformed or confirmed your thoughts?

_____

_____

_____

_____

_____

_____

PRAY

Lord, we long for the day we become unified and
worship you as one people in our distinct ways. Open
the hearts of your children to acknowledge and be
doers of your word, because it is your word that
brings us healing, renewal, and reconciliation. Thank
you for allowing us the opportunity to be in awe of
a world so rich in beauty and diversity. Amen.

Glossary

Discrimination: "Discrimination is the unfair or prejudicial treatment of people and groups based on characteristics such as race, gender, age, or sexual orientation."[1]

Eschatology: The study of future events is often called eschatology, from the Greek word *eschatos*, which means "last." The study of eschatology, then, is the study of "the last things."[2]

Flesh: The flesh and the Spirit are two conflicting forces that exist within the believer. The Spirit is just that—the Holy Spirit. The flesh is the part of the believer that disagrees with the Spirit.

Gentile: A gentile is a person who is not Jewish. The Jews identified gentiles as pagans or worshipers of false gods.

Gospel: "The word itself comes from a Greek word *euangelion*, which literally means 'good news.' In the New Testament, it refers to the announcement that Jesus has brought the reign of God to our world through his life, death, and resurrection from the dead."[3]

Jim Crow Law: "In U.S. history, [Jim Crow law includes] any of the laws that enforced racial segregation in the South between the

1. American Psychological Association, "Discrimination," para. 1.
2. Grudem, *Systematic Theology*, 1091.
3. Mackie, "What Are the Gospels?," para. 2.

end of Reconstruction in 1877 and the beginning of the civil rights movement in the 1950s. *Jim Crow* was the name of a minstrel routine (actually *Jump Jim Crow*) performed beginning in 1828. . . . The term came to be a derogatory epithet for African Americans and a designation for their segregated life."[4]

Judaism: Judaism is a "monotheistic religion developed among the ancient Hebrews. Judaism is characterized by a belief in one transcendent God who revealed himself to Abraham, Moses, and the Hebrew prophets and by a religious life in accordance with Scriptures and rabbinic traditions. Judaism is the complex phenomenon of a total way of life for the Jewish people, comprising theology, law, and innumerable cultural traditions."[5]

Pharisaic: "Practicing or advocating strict observance of external forms and ceremonies of religion or conduct without regard to the spirit; self-righteous; hypocritical."[6]

Samaritan: "The name Samaritans was originally identified with the Northern Kingdom Israelites (2 Kings 17:29). When the Assyrians conquered Israel and exiled 27,290 Israelites, a 'remnant of Israel' remained in the land. Assyrian captives from distant places also settled there (2 Kings 17:24). This led to the intermarriage of some, though not all, Jews with Gentiles and widespread worship of other gods."[7]

---

4. Urofsky, "Jim Crow Law," para. 1.

5. Feldman et al., "Judaism."

6. Dictionary.com, s.v. "pharisaic," https://www.dictionary.com/browse/pharisaic.

7. Potts, *Holman Bible Dictionary*, 1224.

About the Author

DR. JAMES D. CROONE SR. holds a master of arts degree in theology and culture from Northwest University and a doctoral degree in religious education from A. L. Hardy Academy of Theology.

Dr. Croone is an adjunct professor at Northwest University and serves as an executive presbyter with the Northwest Ministry Network in the Seattle area.

In addition, Dr. Croone is the director of the Men's Recovery Program at the Seattle's Union Gospel Mission and pastors Risen Church in the Seattle area (#risenseattle).

He is the author of *Seymour and Parham: The Move of God Amid Relationship and Conflict* (https://www.amazon.com/Seymour-Parham-Move-Relationship-Conflict/dp/1502499762).

Bibliography

American Psychological Association. "Discrimination: What It Is and How to Cope." Last updated May 16, 2024. https://www.apa.org/topics/racism-bias-discrimination/types-stress.

Arnold, Clinton E. *Acts.* Zondervan Illustrated Bible Backgrounds Commentary 2B. Grand Rapids: Zondervan, 2019. Kindle.

Arnold, Clinton E., et al. *Ephesians, Philippians, Colossians, Philemon.* Zondervan Illustrated Bible Backgrounds Commentary. Grand Rapids: Zondervan, 2002. Kindle.

AZ Quotes. "Andrew Young Quotes." https://www.azquotes.com/author/16084-Andrew_Young.

———. "Martin Luther King, Jr.: 'I Was Convinced . . .'" https://www.azquotes.com/quote/501880.

Balentine, Steve. "Biblical Unity." San Gabriel Community Church. May 26, 2011. https://sangabrielcommunity.org/biblical-unity/.

Barton, Bruce, et al. *Life Application New Testament Commentary.* Edited by Philip W. Comfort and Dan Lins. Carol Stream, IL: Tyndale, 2001. Kindle.

Batterson, Mark. "Mark Batterson Quotes." QuoteFancy. https://quotefancy.com/quote/2327199/Mark-Batterson-You-may-be-the-only-Bible-some-people-ever-read-So-the-question-is-Are-you.

Bible.org. "Hatred Between Jews and Samaritans." https://bible.org/illustration/hatred-between-jews-and-samaritans.

Bible Hub. "Pistis." Strong's Lexicon. https://biblehub.com/greek/4102.

Bonhoeffer, Dietrich. *The Cost of Discipleship.* New York: SCM, 1963.

Carter, Joe. "The Countries Where It's Most Dangerous to Be a Christian in 2019." The Gospel Coalition. Jan. 19, 2019. https://www.thegospelcoalition.org/article/the-countries-where-its-most-dangerous-to-be-a-christian-in-2019/.

Clements, Ben. "Three Benefits of Fostering a Multicultural Church." EFAC Australia. Apr. 1, 2022. https://www.efac.org.au/index.php/2022/autumn-2022/three-benefits-of-fostering-a-multicultural-church.

Conner, Sarah. "Martin Luther King Jr. on Complacency." *Paradoxologies* (blog), Aug. 28 2010. https://paradoxologies.org/2010/08/28/martin-luther-king-jr-on-complacency-mlk/.

Deffinbaugh, Bob. "Peter's Capitulation and Paul's Correction." Bible.org. June 28, 2004. https://bible.org/seriespage/peter's-capitulation-and-paul's-correction-galatians-211-21.

Eagleton, Terry. *The Idea of Culture.* Oxford: Oxford University Press, 2000.

Eng, Daniel K. "The Ethnic-Specific Church and MLK's 'Most Segregated Hour' Line." Sola Network. Jan. 20, 2022. https://sola.network/article/ethnic-specific-church-mlk/.

Engelthaler, Lesa. "Three Stories Prove Racial Reconciliation Can Happen (Not Easy)." Missio Alliance. Jan. 31, 2017. https://www.missioalliance.org/three-stories-prove-racial-reconciliation-can-happen-not-easy/.

Feldman, Louis H., et al. "Judaism." *Britannica*, last updated Dec. 31, 2024. https://www.britannica.com/topic/Judaism.

Got Questions. "Who Is My Neighbor, Biblically Speaking?" Last updated Jan. 4, 2022. https://www.gotquestions.org/who-is-my-neighbor.html.

Graham, Billy. "Billy Graham: Do You Bear the Marks of Christ?" *Decision*, Nov. 11, 2019. https://decisionmagazine.com/billy-graham-do-you-bear-marks-christ/#:~:text=You20can20have20the20brand,called20a20followe r20of20Christ.

Grudem, Wayne. *Systematic Theology.* Grand Rapids: Zondervan Academic, 1994. Kindle.

Gundry, Robert H. *A Survey of the New Testament.* 5th ed. Grand Rapids: Zondervan, 2012. Kindle.

Henry, Mary T. "Martin Luther King Jr. Arrives for His Only Seattle Visit on November 8, 1961." History Link. Jan. 8, 1999. https://www.historylink.org/file/673.

Hia, C. P. "The Dividing Wall." Our Daily Bread. Apr. 19, 2011. https://odb.org/2011/04/19/the-dividing-wall.

Horsford, Sonya Douglass. "School Integration in the New Jim Crow: Opportunity or Oxymoron?" *Educational Policy* 33.1 (2019) 257–75. https://doi.org/10.1177/0895904818810526.

Horton, D. A. "Voices with Ed Stetzer: A Missiological Assessment of Critical Race Theory III." Church Leaders. Sept. 23, 2021. https://churchleaders.com/voices/405946-missiological-assessment-of-critical-race-theory.html/4.

Joffe, Lawrence. "Ginetta Sagan." *Guardian*, Sept. 13, 2000. https://www.theguardian.com/news/2000/sep/14/guardianobituaries.

Kaur, Dashmeet. "Is Prejudice a Big Deal?" *Medium*, Feb. 2, 2020. https://dashmeet19.medium.com/is-prejudice-a-big-deal-a9efob78d53b.

Keller, Timothy. *Generous Justice: How God's Grace Makes Us Just.* New York: Penguin, 2016. Kindle.

Kennedy, Stetson. *Jim Crow Guide: The Way It Was.* Boca Raton: Florida Atlantic University Press, 1990.

King, Martin Luther, Jr., *Stride Toward Freedom: The Montgomery Story*. Boston: Beacon, 1958.

Longley, Robert. "What Is Multiculturalism? Definition, Theories, and Examples." ThoughtCo. July 23, 2024. https://www.thoughtco.com/what-is-multiculturalism-4689285.

MacArthur, John. *ESV MacArthur Study Bible*. Wheaton, IL: Crossway, 2018. Kindle.

Mackie, Tim. "What Are the Gospels? The Answer Is Far More Exciting and Complex Than We've Been Led to Believe." BibleProject. Aug. 27, 2017. https://bibleproject.com/blog/what-are-the-gospels/.

McLaughlin, Rebecca. *Confronting Christianity: 12 Hard Questions for the World's Largest Religion*. Wheaton, IL: Crossway, 2019.

Moo, Douglas J., et al. *Romans, Galatians*. Zondervan Illustrated Bible Backgrounds Commentary. Grand Rapids: Zondervan Academic. Kindle.

Morrison, Latasha. *Be the Bridge: Pursuing God's Heart for Racial Reconciliation*. Colorado Springs: WaterBrook, 2019.

———. "June 2020—Pursue Racial Reconciliation." IF. June 2020. https://www.ifgathering.com/iftable-legacy/pursue-racial-reconciliation/.

Naselli, Andrew David. "2 Corinthians 5:16." *NIV Biblical Theology Study Bible: Follow God's Redemptive Plan as It Unfolds Throughout Scripture*, edited by D. A. Carson. Grand Rapids: Zondervan, 2018. Kindle.

Nelson, Thomas. *NKJV Hebrew-Greek Key Word Study Bible: Bringing the Original Text to Life*. Chattanooga, TN: AMG, 2015.

Pediaa. "Difference Between Assimilation and Acculturation." Sept. 11, 2015. https://pediaa.com/difference-between-assimilation-and-acculturation/.

Perkins, John M. "162 Racial Equality Quotes to Inspire You." Quotelr. July 4, 2024. https://quotlr.com/quotes-about-racial-equality.

Pisters, Siri. "Reflections on Diversity and the Risk of Creating Boundaries." Susplace. Nov. 2, 2016. https://www.sustainableplaceshaping.net/reflections-on-diversity-and-the-risk-of-creating-boundaries/.

Ponio, Judy. "What We Can Learn from the Good Samaritan Story." Our Father's House Soup Kitchen. July 13, 2023. https://ofhsoupkitchen.org/good-samaritan-life-today.

Potts, Donald R. *Holman Bible Dictionary*. Edited by Trent C. Butler. Nashville: Holman Bible, 1991.

Powell, Frank. "12 Signs You Are a Modern-Day Pharisee." *Frank Powell* (blog), Oct. 14, 2014. https://frankpowell.me/13-signs-pharisee-follower-jesus/.

Raboteau, Albert. *Slave Religion: The "Invisible Institution" in the Antebellum South*. Rev. ed. New York: Oxford University Press, 2004. Kindle.

Raftery, Isolde. "Martin Luther King Workshopped His 'I Have a Dream' Speech in Seattle." KUOW, Jan. 20, 2019. https://www.kuow.org/stories/what-martin-luther-king-jr-told-seattle-the-one-time-he-visited.

Rand, W. W. "Justice." *American Tract Society Bible Dictionary*. 1859. https://www.studylight.org/dictionaries/eng/ats/j/justice.html.

Sanz, Catherine. "Police Officer Comforts 5-Year-Old Girl at George Floyd Protest." ABC News, June 5, 2020. https://abcnews.go.com/

GMA/Family/police-officer-comforts-year-girl-george-floyd-protest/ story?id=71086097.

Seedbed. "Xavier's Powerful Story About Race and Reconciliation: Awakening Stories." Apr. 2, 2019. https://seedbed.com/xaviers-powerful-story-about-race-and-reconciliation-awakening-stories/.

Smith, Shaun. "Acts 6 Teaches True Leadership: Leadership Was Chosen by the 'Brothers and Sisters,' Not from the Top Down." *Musings from Under the Bus* (blog), June 24, 2014. https://musingsfromunderthebus.wordpress. com/2014/06/24/acts-6-teaches-true-leadership-leadership-was-chosen-by-the-brothers-and-sisters-not-from-the-top-down/.

Songfacts. "I Walk the Line by Johnny Cash." https://www.songfacts.com/facts/ johnny-cash/i-walk-the-line.

Strauss, Mark L. "The Parable of the Good Samaritan (10:25–37)." In *Matthew, Mark, Luke*, edited by Clinton E. Arnold. Zondervan Illustrated Bible Backgrounds Commentary 1. Grand Rapids: Zondervan, 2019. Kindle.

Syverson, Jeff. "Faithful to the Unfaithful." *pastor jeff's neighborhood* (blog), Dec. 5, 2023. https://pastorjeffs.blog/2023/12/05/faithful-to-the-unfaithful-4/.

Urofsky, Melvin I. "Jim Crow Law." *Britannica*, Dec. 29, 2023. https://www. britannica.com/event/Jim-Crow-law.

Vinney, Cynthia. "Status Quo Bias: What It Means and How It Affects Your Behavior." ThoughtCo. Dec. 11, 2019. https://www.thoughtco.com/status-quo-bias-4172981.

Williams, Marvin, and Al Lopus. "A True Story of Prejudice, Forgiveness, and True Reconciliation." Best Christian Workplaces. June 23, 2020. https:// workplaces.org/articles/flourish-factor/healthy-communication/a-true-story-of-prejudice-forgiveness-and-true-reconciliation.

Winkler, Alice. "'I Walk the Line.'" *All Things Considered*, NPR, Dec. 23, 2000. https://www.npr.org/2000/12/23/1115971/npr-100-i-walk-the-line.

Youngblood, Ronald F., ed. *Nelson's Illustrated Bible Dictionary*. Nashville: Thomas Nelson, 2014. Kindle.